Ger

JAZZ MASTERS SERIES

Gerry Mulligan's Ark

RAYMOND HORRICKS

Selected Discography by
Tony Middleton

To my godson, David Smith

Once I promised you a book. But then in between my daughter wanted another one for herself. So, I hope you will come to like what I have written here instead.

Also for Rosemarie and Ray Swinfield.

First published in Great Britain in 1986 by
APOLLO PRESS LIMITED
11 Baptist Gardens, London NW5 4ET

© Raymond Horricks 1986

British Library Cataloguing in Publication Data
Horricks, Raymond
  Gerry Mulligan.—(Jazz masters series; 12)
  1. Mulligan, Gerry 2. Saxophonists—
  United States—Biography
  I. Title II. Middleton, Tony III. Series
  788'.66'0924 ML419.M/

ISBN 0-948820-01-2

Series editor: David Burnett James

Typesetting by Concept Communications, Crayford, Kent

Printed and Bound in Great Britain by
Anchor Brendon Limited, Tiptree, Essex

Contents

Acknowledgements

As usual I begin by thanking my discographer, Tony Middleton. That I have grown to know his patience and careful research doesn't make his task any easier. But in Mulligan's case it becomes a positive nightmare. I can't think of any other major figure in the history of jazz who has got in on a wider variety of sessions, or as many.

A number of musicians have helped me, and they have been credited at appropriate points in the text.

However, I owe an especial debt of gratitude to Gordon Jack of South London. He too is a baritone-player and, I discovered, owns *everything* that has been issued by Gerry Mulligan on record, plus many airshots, etc. (I have tried to do the same with the pianist Bill Evans, who died prematurely and in any case was a less-prolific recording artist than Mulligan. And I'm still failing; so I understand why Gordon's collection is unique.) Anyway, when he heard that the book was under way he immediately offered his help, which has proved to be invaluable, both in loaning me tapes of items I could not otherwise obtain and in supplying information relevant to certain parts of the manuscript.

R.H.
Senegal/England, 1986

The publishers thank Roy Burchell and *Melody Maker* for access to their files.

Illustrations

Gerry Mulligan. Photo: Tim Motion

Chapter One

Any artist grows into a public figure through being always willing to address strangers.

Of the many people, probably millions, certainly countless thousands, who have enjoyed being brought into an awareness of Gerry Mulligan's music only a tiny proportion will have met the man himself. Not that that really matters. Many will have seen him with his groups and his orchestra in clubs or at concerts. Others, in fact many more in their far-flung outposts, will be the custodians of one or several or even most of his records. All of them feel however that they do know this man *because of the music which exists.*

Such is the inherent, individual character of each of the major exponents of jazz that, not only are they instantly recognizable, but in collaboration with their source materials they can communicate with an audience at every possible cerebral and emotional level. Not just 'in person', when the atmosphere is likely to be charged with premature warmth. Even via the disembodied flatness of a tape or a disc.

Mulligan is also a person who lives in spurts and appears to keep living, creatively, by the fire of his intelligence. Again, this is only to be expected of an outstanding artist. For what is important is to ensure that out of a period devoted to strict mental retreat the new is forthcoming. Mulligan's overall output is not yet something to be observed through a sheet of glass in a museum. He is still very much of this world.

In reality his sensibilities are as modern as their perimeters. Which means that his personal Ark is still sailing on into uncharted waters. But, unlike Noah's, it stops every so often on its voyaging to pick up a fresh crew; also while its captain hoists the extra sail on his latest batch of playing and writing. Even so: it is now steered with immense knowledge and experience — and cargoed with absolute ability.

His career in jazz has in one sense come full circle. He started out (publicly) with big bands, then made a name for himself with several of the most distinguished smaller and small groups of the late 1940s, the early 1950s and on through into the 1960s; including the Miles Davis nine-piecer and his own West Coast-based pianoless Quartet with trumpeter Chet Baker — later replaced by valve-trombonist Bob Brookmeyer. Now, from the later 1970s and into the 1980s he has had a permanent big band of his own, albeit completely different in all except instrumentation to those for whom he first played and wrote.

Often, the going has been decidedly rough, but in the main Mulligan has avoided the worst traps of his chosen profession: the greed, the complacency, the alarms of impending musical impotence. Instead he has found and rested briefly on the Mount Ararat of success — but preferring then to let his Ark's journey continue. The rocks and whirlpools of an artistic life as T.S.Eliot refers to them in *The Dry Salvages* are now mostly left behind:

> 'We cannot think of a time that is oceanless
> Or of an ocean not littered with wastage
> Or of a future that is not liable
> Like the past, to have no destination.'

For this is certainly not true of the latest travelling by Mulligan's music. And I think it is only fair to stress that his Ark has no unnecessary residue of crustaceans clinging to its underside. But one line from Eliot's 'Four Quartets' can be applied to him absolutely: *His rhythm was present in the nursery bedroom.*

The real 'Dry Salvages' of jazz are sloppiness, in effect the taking of the music for granted; or not having a proper objective in the first place. Mulligan could not possibly be accused of either of these. Even his former personal problems never interrupted the musical output; his blend of idealism with the drive for fulfilment. Artists engrossed in working out their creative destinies are compelled to make an assault on perfection, otherwise they become their own dupes and, as self-flatterers, their contributions are no more beneficial than pulling

10

Gerry Mulligan.

up handfuls of carrots. With his 'Ark/Orchestra' of recent years Gerry Mulligan has achieved a new kind of maturity — as a double instrumentalist, as a leader of men (plus one woman) and yet again as a reaffirmed writer of music. However, this present state of affairs also involves curiosity, a spirit of adventure and, in the final analysis, some courage. Perhaps this last ingredient is the most important of all — and what has kept him to the fore in contemporary jazz. 'Courage is not simply *one* of the virtues but the form of every virtue at the testing point, which means at the point of highest reality.' (C.S.Lewis)

He has also, over the years, gained immeasurably in self-confidence with his music. When I first met and spoke with him — in Paris in 1954 — despite the many fascinations of his then-pianoless Quartet there was a kind of youthful gawkiness about his movements upon the stage, emphasized by a severe crew-cut and a rather baggy silk suit. Again, later that same evening, I stood in between Jack Parnell and trumpeter Jonah Jones listening to an extraordinary jam session when Thelonious Monk crashed chords with Mulligan's Quartet. Again — once he got the gist of what was going on — Gerry blew his horn magnificently, but otherwise he seemed shy and diffident; and when his wife of those years said bossily they ought to go back to their hotel he meekly packed the baritone away and accompanied her. And that appeared to be that. Success and acclaim he now had — but its mantle was not draped too comfortably around his shoulders. At the same time though I still had in my head all of his previous, exceedingly precocious writing — for Gene Krupa and Elliot Lawrence and Stan Kenton and Miles Davis, plus his solos with and conception for the Quartet, and I knew there was real courage in his music.

In contrast. . . at the Nice Jazz Festival in 1982 we were confronted by an almost entirely different Mulligan — sure, secure in front of his superb ensemble and a man at the peak of his own audacity. He was smartly turned out in a frilled shirt and black trousers; he conducted with *panache,* flourished his baritone (and the later-acquired soprano) with dandyish theatricality and encouraged his younger players with an overt authority.

He showed authority too in dealing with certain members of the sound-rigging team in the Roman arena at Cimiez we had for that particular Nice. In fact, he had arrived at the airport only to be told there would be no time for a sound-balance before the first concert. Gerry blew his top! 'My Orchestra deserves to be heard properly,' he said angrily. 'No sound-rehearsal, then *no* performance!' Following which he got his way. This in itself was perfectly correct, because if some of the riggers were okay for 'pop' festivals, they were not competent when it came to jazz; and why singer Carmen McRae at a subsequent concert, having also suffered and in response to unanimous audience demand, pointed out that her encore number might be considered appropriate: *Send In The Clowns.*

I had arrived up the hill at Cimiez early for the Mulligan evening and I took a photograph of the shambles which attended the beginning of his rehearsal: with the sound-riggers in total disarray, Gerry's pianist hand-on-hip shaking his head in total disbelief and Gerry himself just about to take over. In the end he re-positioned the microphones himself — and discarded several of them altogether. 'My musicians have their own internal balance,' was his firm comment. 'We don't need half of this ridiculous paraphernalia just to make you guys look important.' The subject was closed. Only to be reopened when the orchestra played that night, thrilling everyone in the arena with its marvellous mix of ensemble and solos. The repertoire just flowed: *For An Unfinished Woman, Song For Strayhorn, Walk On The Water* and the ovations began to rise to the sky. Gerry even — and the listeners loved it — stopped one piece a chorus in and adjusted the mouthpiece to his baritone. He had not been happy with the intonation. The audience accepted his desire and pursuit of the whole; the search for excellence. . .

As a musician Mulligan is a man of many parts. As a jazz musician he belongs to a select few which would also include Benny Carter (once dubbed 'The Cat With Nine Lives') and the late Eric Dolphy, the great new multiple talent of the 1960s, a man who has not been content to shine in one jazz sphere, say a virtuoso instrumental role like Louis Armstrong, but feels compelled to move in others as well.

He is a virtuoso soloist on baritone-saxophone, a fine player on soprano-saxophone (recently), an adequate but interesting pianist, one of the best, most distinctive and original composers jazz has known, and an accomplished arranger to follow these composing abilities through. In addition he has pioneered at least three, and possibly four of the most significant stylistic developments in jazz. At the same time though he is very much a person of the music's middle-ground, who progresses the individualities of his own creativity without seeking to be deliberately 'way out'. He loves Ellington, Strayhorn and many earlier players and composers, and as such — although obviously a product of modern jazz in the 1940s — he is a natural extension to the main stream of evolution. Certain so-called *avant garde* reputations have already fallen by the wayside. Mulligan's will not, because he contains *all* the great jazz traditions, the truly 'classic' qualities, as well as the surprises of modernism.

One further thing requires to be said at this point. The different parts of Mulligan's music interlock as in a highly superior jigsaw. The memorable melodic lines of his compositions appear as the logical outcome of how he plays the baritone, and in turn the compositions themselves suggest the direction his arranging will then take. His various groups, and now his Orchestra, have been a necessary shop-window, but always easily identifiable with the man.

Chapter Two

He was born under Aries, first sign of the Zodiac, on 6 April 1927 in Queens Village, Long Island, New York and christened *Gerald Joseph*. ('Gerry' is the original family form of address. Later certain musicians would re-nickname him 'Jeru'.) For those who believe in astrology Aries has come to be regarded as the ignition-key of the Zodiac and those who belong to it as both headlong and headstrong. True or false, the young Mulligan was certainly precocious with regard to music. He grew up in various places, but then in Philadelphia, less than two hours by train from New York and a city with a very strong jazz tradition of its own. By his late 'teens he was already writing his first arrangements, influenced by Duke Ellington, the big Swing bands and what he had heard of early be-bop, and of course Lester Young. At the same time, however, he was determined to be his own man, and to open up new possibilities.

As indeed he was with the baritone-saxophone, an instrument he had opted for even before his writing experiments. 'In a way, I started out to be a baritone-player,' he explains. 'My problem, as a youth, was that I couldn't afford one. So I started on clarinet. Then I had an alto while I saved up to buy the baritone. My first jobs were mainly single engagements, club dates and that sort of thing, on alto and tenor. Until I got the bigger horn.'

This being pre-Charlie Parker, Mulligan's own instrumental influences were fairly diverse. 'As a kid,' he remembers, 'I heard records by Adrian Rollini on the even bigger bass-saxophone. My family bought records by Red Nichols (hence Gerry's version of

Left to right: Wes Fisher, Gerry Mulligan (Aged 16), Robert Weiss.

Varsity Drag), Paul Whiteman and stuff like that. I hadn't been overly aware of them. I realised the influence later. For what Rollini did with that horn melodically was beautiful. He approached it in a linear way. Twenty years later when I heard those records again I was stunned. I said: *Gee whiz — I thought we had dreamed up something new here*! I took a lesson from Adrian Rollini.

'Of course Rollini was a generation before Lester Young, and I know he, Prez, was influenced a great deal by Bud Freeman. It never occurred to me to ask Prez about Adrian Rollini, but I have a hunch that he loved his playing. Even in those days, he was running up and down the chords and making melodies out of them. He must have been a tremendous influence on the guys he played with. Actually, when I was very young . . . and began listening to saxophones, I was first attracted to Coleman Hawkins. And loving the way Hawk played made me listen to a bunch of marvellous tenor players of that period. It was really quite a bit later, after I'd been playing with bands already, that I heard Lester. In fact I heard Bird (Charlie Parker) first, and had got well into listening to him. You know, it's the kind of accidental thing that awareness of a player is: what's available, what somebody happens to play for you.

'Prez made things clear to me. It was like opening up new, simple vistas that were always there; but it took Prez to make those simple things obvious. Prez was such a lovely songwriter. Everything he played was a song, you know. And his sense of rhythm, and way he laid his songs over the surrounding music; he did it with such a flowing sense of ease. I'd come to understand 'soaring' from Bird, but Prez's kind of soaring I didn't know about. And when I listened back to Bird, and I realised he knew all *about* that. In the end, that's the thing that knocks me out about all of the players I've ever loved — they're basically songwriters. They love melody. This is hard to fit in with what some people are thinking now; what we think of as a conventional melody is a kind of dirty word. I can't have any sort of feeling towards that attitude. I like what I hear other guys doing, but the thing that really attracts me is melodic playing.

'Miles Davis is another one who writes songs when he plays. And the irony is that he is now in the vanguard of putting melodies down. Although one can never tell with Miles; he's really one of the great camp characters of all time. But if you're lyrically and melodically orientated — as Miles is — you can do *anything*. Because if you've got the wit, you can make anything into a melody, ultimately.'

Gerry has more to say on the subject of the modern Miles which forcefully ties in with his perfectionist behaviour as I witnessed it at Nice '82. 'In recent years, I haven't heard him (Miles) much in person. But if he's dropped that muted sound, I'll have to admit to being delighted. To me that was the same kind of thing — like putting someone on. I've always wanted to say: "Miles, wait a minute — I must not get sucked into this particular thing. Because I think you're putting somebody on, and it may be *me!*" I thought this business of putting a harmon-mute right into a microphone didn't ring true. I don't like the sound. You're dealing with a mechanical device; when you put that mute into it, the air vibrates against the diaphragm in the mike and distorts. Now, there's a whole area of music going on today where people are dealing with electronic distortion. *But if I could I'd rather work without microphones altogether.*'

Prior to this the baritone-saxophone had gained a decidedly cumbersome image in jazz. Duke Ellington had featured Harry Carney playing it of course; but this was to give his scores added texture and depth, exploiting the baritone's rich sonorities. Mulligan admired Carney's sound and his accurate phrasing, but as he grew more adept with the instrument himself he realised its greater potentialities. How its range could be better utilised to produce a brighter, airier sound for instance; also that it was possible to play much faster on it and with more daring ideas than had been visualised previously. If Charlie Parker could do such remarkable things with the alto-saxophone then surely the baritone was ripe for a new assessment as well. As Gerry himself points out, 'There are so many things you can do with a baritone. You can cross-voice it with 'cellos, French horns, all the low instruments; also you can relate it with higher voices if you want to. You don't really have that facility with the alto and tenor'. Ironically, what Gerry did *not* know at this moment was that he had an unknown rival in such thinking. Serge Chaloff, whose father played with the Boston Symphony Orchestra, was even now trying to play like Charlie Parker on the baritone — and would later, briefly, come to be regarded as ahead of everyone with the instrument.

Mulligan got his first professional work as an arranger with a band led by one Johnny Warrington at WCAU, Philadelphia's local radio station. This in turn brought him to the attention of Elliot Lawrence, leader of the station's 'house' band. Lawrence recognised his talent — and all the signs of a growing individuality. Soon Gerry was writing for him on a regular basis. Mostly he was called on to arrange popular songs: *Bye Bye Blackbird, But Not For Me, My Silent Love.* But Lawrence also accepted the first Mulligan originals, *Rocker* and *The Happy Hooligan.* What impressed him so much about these and other scores (and remember Gerry was still under twenty) was not just the sure handling of thematic materials but at the same time the intelligent background writing to solo passages. Plus of course the way they lent themselves to swing. Clearly the young man knew exactly what he wanted to say and how to say it. . .

It was partly due to its superior scores that in the summer of 1946 the Lawrence band received an attractive offer to play at New York's Stadtler Hotel. Mulligan went with it. A significant move for it meant that at last he could meet, and sometimes play with, the leading luminaries of modern jazz. And write for other bands, most notably in 1946/47 Gene Krupa's. This was the group which included Red Rodney and the Triscari brothers (trumpets), Buddy Wise and Charlie Ventura (tenor saxophones) and Teddy Napoleon (piano),

18

and was an excellent showcase for any aspiring arranger because Krupa himself was very much a national figure, both as a drummer and bandleader. Gerry did not get to play baritone with the band for quite some time. And even in his writing he could not be entirely himself on account of the accepted Krupa sound and style. But he penned an exciting version of *How High The Moon*. (Even if the beat is still straight 4/4 time, all the solos are boppish and so are the ensembled variations.) While Gene also agreed to record another Mulligan original, *Disc Jockey Jump*. This is untypical Mulligan writing by comparison with his later linear style; nevertheless its essentially Swing-style phrases are skilfully arranged and the theme became very popular with Krupa's audiences. (The resulting record is additionally noteworthy for a fine trumpet solo by Don Fagerquist.)

At which point re-enter Serge Chaloff.

There is no doubt that Mulligan's next logical step after Krupa would have been to join the great new 1947 Herman Herd, the famous 'Four Brothers' band. I say this especially because of his natural affinities, stylistically that is, both as a player and writer, with its other membership — with Stan Getz, Zoot Sims, Shorty Rogers, Don Lamond, Bill Bauer, Chubby Jackson, Jimmy Giuffre *et al*, all of whom he would work with on later projects. However, by this time Chaloff was very much regarded as *the* modern exponent of the baritone. He was agile, he was often wildly exciting to listen to, and — equally important — he had been heard along New York's 52nd Street jamming with some of the best — Parker, Gillespie, Allen Eager, all the respected figures. The remainder of his life was to be hectic, drug-ridden and comparatively brief, eventually ending in a wheel-chair with spinal paralysis. But in 1947 he landed the baritone-chair with Woody Herman. Which in turn changed Gerry Mulligan's life, because he now settled for the apparently quieter haven of the Claude Thornhill Orchestra, resulting in a musical metamorphosis.

It is probably true that Chaloff had the edge on Mulligan as an instrumentalist at this stage, although he would never be able to equal the latter's lyricism. Gerry meanwhile was working very hard and could handle the big horn with increasing grace and flexibility. His tone too had developed, tempering Harry Carney's basically vibrato-laden sound with many subtle softnesses and attention to dynamics. It was a purer, calmer tone than had been heard before from the baritone in jazz. The sound definitely had to complement whatever were the improvised ideas and resultant phrases now.

But the real metamorphosis occurred within his approach to composing and arranging. For with the Thornhill band he encountered a very different concept of music-making, and first became acquainted with a fellow-arranger of genius in Gil Evans. The Thornhill sound, although the band itself played 'society' functions, was based on some intricate, complicated textures — while the instrumentation included French horns, multiple woodwind, two baritones and a tuba. Evans, half a generation older than Mulligan, was the architect of the band's best scores. Admittedly, several of these were built upon fast be-bop themes. Others, though, involved innovation of a most daring nature: his voicing unusual combinations of instruments, for instance, then continually shifting the textures, and above all his playing fast and loose with formerly rigid bar-lines. Apart from liking Gil personally, Mulligan had found in him a kindred spirit. Their individual work would always show up differences. (Such as Gil's nearly always entrusting his main experiments at this period to the brasses, whereas Gerry — predictably because one himself — would turn increasingly with his to the saxophone players.) No matter. They still had much in common. And not least an interest in the more flowing form of orchestral development instead of the hard vertical forms of previous jazz.

Soon they were meeting up regularly in Gil's manuscript-littered apartment on West 55th Street (behind a Chinese laundry) to debate where exactly the new jazz ought to be going. And other modernists began to drop by. Altoist Lee Konitz, also from the Thornhill band and the most important new man on his chosen instrument since Charlie Parker; trombonist Kai Winding; and of course, the trumpeter Miles Davis. Plus the composer/arrangers Johnny Carisi, George Russell and John Lewis. 'We were musically attracted to each other,' Evans recalls. 'The other arrangers and I. The way we influenced each other was not of so much importance. I feel we kept our own individuality through having each other as musical colleagues rather than by having a common platform or working alone.' Nevertheless these men were the perpetrators of what came to be labelled 'cool' jazz as distinct from the frantic pace of early be-bop. They were influenced by the sounds and textures of Thornhill together with the melodic introspection of Lennie Tristano's group, within which Lee Konitz interwove quietly creative lines with fellow-saxist Warne Marsh. But they were still swinging.

The distillation of all their thinking brought about the now legendary Miles Davis nine-piece band of 1948/49 (the 'Birth Of The Cool' band as headlined on Capitol Records' reissue of the main tracks). I have already written about the importance — as well as the trials and tribulations — of this unit in an earlier book, *Svengali, Or The Orchestra Called Gil Evans*. But since Mulligan became a major contributor to its music and eventual influence a few small repetitions are necessary in describing the role he played. Also, while his composing and arranging remain uppermost here, at the same time the recordings reveal a first flowering of his work on baritone.

I once said that Gerry's composing over this period was by 'a greatly gifted miniaturist', his themes being brief and easy to pick up; but there can be no doubting his big leap forward as an arranger, creating charts which are full of surprises. Without being a power-house group the front line needed depth. Miles wanted a rich, full sound, mellow in its unison voicings, but prepared for contrapuntal effects within the subsequent passages. The baritone, French horn and tuba increased the depth, therefore, and the arrangers had a total range of more than three and a half octaves. In the overall voicing the complement of lighter and deep-toned instruments was perfectly balanced. The ensemble sound was varied considerably by the redistribution of lead parts, with plenty of room to stress 'light and shade': in other words, the essential dynamics of music. Meanwhile the melody instruments were never too unwieldy and could swing along quite easily with the rhythm section.

For Miles's first recording session (on 21 January 1949) Gerry scored two pieces: *Godchild*, a theme by pianist George Wallington, and his own composition *Jeru*. With *Godchild* he immediately raises the curtain on the group's ensemble range. The theme has an ascending main phrase, and his score opens with the tuba, the deepest voice, playing lead but then moves up through the lighter-sounding instruments until the trumpet seems to fly out from the top of the ensemble. Miles must have been very impressed by this design, for he flows on from the written line into one of his most intense and inventive solos. It is also interesting to note from the performance how Mulligan has determined to obtain a flexible exposure of the composition. For the final thirty-two bars, instead of repeating the opening chorus, he has written a new thematic statement — with an entirely different melody built over Wallington's original chords. In contrast, *Jeru* is a simple swinger with a light saxophone voicing and smoothly-riding phrases. The supple movement of the ensemble is underlined by Max Roach's superb open cymbal work and the whole band sounds in complete accord. Even so, there are still innovations, like the insertion of several bars in 3/4 time to emphasise the predominance of the 4/4.

The date didn't pass off easily though. 'We'd been rehearsing for what *seemed* like a year,' Gerry recalls. 'It was a labour of love with everybody concerned. We did it because we wanted to do it. Capitol sent along Pete Rugolo as the A & R man, to supervise the date. They felt that, as another composer and arranger, he'd be able to record the band well. I'll never forget the first break we took, after we'd been working for an hour or so; they were still trying to get the sound together.

'I couldn't understand why they were having such a problem recording this thing. It was so straightforward; we got a balance between ourselves. I'd known Pete a long time with Stan Kenton's band, and in the break he took me aside and said: "*Listen, I don't know what kind of sound you guys are going for.*" I said to him: "*What's the difficulty? You're trying to record the guys individually; you should be recording the ensemble as a whole, and saving yourself a lot of trouble.*" It was a shock to me that the guys in the control-room had no idea what we were doing. It seemed so simple and totally logical to us. I mean, it's like, all instruments are there to use all the time. We'd figured out an instrumentation that worked for our purposes: the smallest possible ensemble to give the most possibilities for the writers to work with.'

For the 22 April 1949 Davis session Gerry contributed only one score, his own original *Venus De Milo*. But it is an important one, because it gives evidence of the longer lines he would now increasingly introduce into his compositions as distinct from the short, succinct phrases of his earlier themes. Moreover it is an attractive melody line in itself and again inspires Miles to create a very fine solo, with Gerry cleverly varying the ensemble backing.

For the band's final session on 9 March 1950 he provided a reworking of his *Rocker*, another 32-bar theme with the main eight revolving around a reiterated three-note phrase. Once more the arranger builds a second theme over the chord sequence. He features

Gerry Mulligan, Art Farmer and Bill Crow

it in a central ensemble passage, then breaks the pattern with eight bars of solo baritone leading to a recapitulation of the original melody. But by this time the band was washed up, finished — so that the session is more in the nature of an obituary. (In so far as Capitol was concerned, it 'tidied' the contractual situation. . .) Up against the more easily grasped excitements of Dizzy Gillespie's big band the Davis group had been a complete flop in public (they lasted only two weeks at New York's Royal Roost), and it would take years before their records were fully appreciated — except, that is, by a number of more discerning other musicians.

Gerry took the blow harder than most. He had had high hopes of their particular concept in jazz becoming successful; now it meant starting again. Although not quite, for he was showing considerable advancement as a writer, and on baritone it was generally accepted that at last he led the field.

He tried to keep a group going with Kai Winding, tenorman Brew Moore and George Wallington on piano. Usually the bass player was

Tommy Potter, with Roy Haynes on drums, and they recorded a number of titles issued mostly under Winding's name but with two under Brew Moore's. But publicly this venture failed as well and by the end of the year (1949) he was back with Elliot Lawrence, arranging and playing in a small group drawn from the band. He also recorded with Chubby Jackson (including his longest baritone solo so far on *I May Be Wrong*). And he did several things for the Prestige label's 'New Sounds' series when such new Mulligan compositions as *Roundhouse, Funhouse* and *Mullenium* were first introduced.

But it was with the two scores he wrote for the Lawrence band that Gerry most impressed me over this interim period. Harold Arlen's *Between The Devil And The Deep Blue Sea*, although written as a popular song, has exactly the kind of melodic line which fits the arranger's growing conviction that he must proceed along a more 'horizontal' course; and the arrangement benefits as a result. His own *Elevation* is — I believe — his best actual composition thus far. It still has a kind of early be-bop quality about the fastness and intricacy of the phrasing, while at the same time drawing in his awareness that the contours of a theme should flow *and appear to be flowing somewhere*. In this case it is into good solos, most notably by tenorman Phil Urso (Gerry himself did not play on the date). Even in his writing for the brasses there is an obvious desire to escape from the fixed groupings associated with the Swing era and which would continue up to and including the early Kenton. Saxophones still dominate the theme statement, but there is a genuine attempt to make up different mixes of instruments and then even to make the brass punctuations move along in a linear style as well. Overall there is a retained swing and general excitement, just to prove the exponents of so-called 'cool' jazz were not all locked up in ivory towers.

Towards the end of the arrangement Gerry has both the saxophones and the brasses playing melodic lines around each other instead of merely swapping 4 or 8-bar passages: another significant development. For by this time, and through knowing Lee Konitz, Gerry had absorbed much of what had been happening within the Lennie Tristano workshop. In particular the weaving and interweaving of lines. Counterpoint, as first properly defined by J.S.Bach and others, had been largely absent from jazz music since the freely-improvised playing of the New Orleans bands. The big Swing bands had opted for their brass and reed sections alternating in harmonised 'blocks', while the early be-boppers had relied upon a unison-ensembled frontline attack. But playing with Tristano, Konitz and Warne Marsh had brought improvised counterpoint back into jazz — with the added sophistication of its being based on the instrumental devices of be-bop. One must remember too that Konitz was looked upon by many musicians as the principal alto player on the New York scene by the later 1940s. I will not argue the rights or wrongs of this; but Charlie Parker, the revolutionary genius of early modern jazz, had become increasingly ill and unreliable. Lee's alternative, playing variations on a given theme with the quiet depths as of a lily-pond but still swinging could hardly have failed to impress the now-rapidly maturing Mulligan. But probably his interweavings with Warne Marsh impressed the arranger even more. If two men could do it, why not whole groupings of jazzmen? Or, better still, why not set up three and four lines of parallel counterpoint to create a genuine *Concerto Grosso* effect?

Peter Ind, the London-born bass-player, took up residence in New York around this time — the first British musician after George Shearing to do so. And as a result of joining the Tristano experiments, he got to know Mulligan fairly well. He confirms that Gerry was 'always around, always aware, absorbing, and attempting everything on his horn. He was good in the company of other musicians,' Ind goes on, 'but I realised there was an edge to him at this time, an inner tension. Of course, we were all scuffling. Every other day someone would ask me to lend them a dollar. Or I would them! Also Gerry had this personal problem then. Which required more money and therefore became a social problem for him as well. Okay, so lots of the guys got hooked. Some got off it, others didn't. But the price on the street was high, and work was scarce. All the old be-bop haunts along 52nd Street had closed, the places where before you could hear Diz, Bird, Coleman Hawkins, Max Roach, all of those people.
'Anyway, then I fell into a rehearsal situation with Gerry. He'd begun to play really well on the baritone, and in the right mood he loved to do a little jamming. Other times though the truly serious side showed. He was often very down, disillusioned because what he'd tried so hard to do with Miles and so on hadn't gained ground. So he tried once more — and this was the start of the idea of his having a pianoless quartet. It began at Nola's Studios, now a big modern

complex but then a grotty, run-down place where musicians could rehearse for one, maybe two dollars an hour. And Gerry began to work there without a piano. I often played bass with him at these rehearsals. Sometimes there'd be Al Levitt from the Tristano setup on drums. Together with a variety of trumpet-players — Don Ferrara, Don Joseph, Jerry Lloyd. Others too. The concept showed a lot of promise and Gerry had started writing a bunch of new themes. But when he tried to sell the idea to bookers and the New York recording companies they just didn't want to know. I think that was what finished him about the East (Coast) . . . the last straw. In 1952 he headed for California.'

Chapter Three

'The instruments of music are made ready,
Strong wine is in our cups;
Flute-songs flutter, to a din of magic drums.
Sound scuds and scatters, surges free as a flood . . .'

—*Arthur Waley*
'Chinese Poems'

Alan Watts makes a statement in his book *The Way Of Zen* which is particularly apt as regards the life of a jazz musician. 'The meaning of worth and success in terms of time,' he says, 'and the insistent demand for assurances of a promising future, make it impossible to live freely both in the present and in the 'promising' future when it arrives. For there is never anything but the present, and if one cannot live there, one cannot live anywhere.'

Suddenly, by the early 1950s for many musicians the jazz 'present' and the springboard for many things became California. The failure of Parker and Gillespie at Billy Berg's in Hollywood in 1946 was now just a bad memory. For white musicians in particular Los Angeles had become a hive of activity.

Actually the division (in the early 1950s) of second-generation modernists into a black school of New York and a white school of the West Coast was not quite the conscious separation of the races it might appear. In fact, it was not even a complete separation. White jazzmen continued to work in the East: Stan Getz, Jimmy Raney, Al Haig; while Wardell Gray worked 'out West', likewise Benny Carter,

Harry Edison and Britt Woodman (prior to the latter's joining Duke Ellington); and pianist Hampton Hawes was also there. Economic factors as much as anything contributed to the split. The younger black musician found he could make a living playing with quintets and sextets in the Eastern clubs. The good white one discovered he could make more money in California, either in big bands like Stan Kenton's or working in film and TV studios. It corresponded too with a desire on the part of many white jazzmen to add to their formal knowledge: initially by study, but later in experiments with jazz and the devices of modern European music. And the West Coast had many reputable colleges and music centres. (Darius Milhaud was teaching at Mills in Oakland, for instance.)

The best-known 'founder fathers' of the West Coast school were trumpeter/composer/arranger Shorty Rogers and drummer Shelly Manne. Both had passed through the Kenton 'Innovations' orchestra of 1950, while Shorty had been commissioned to write for Kenton (*Jolly Rogers*, *Viva Prado* and the concert-length *Art Pepper*). But they gradually veered away from this setting. Stan wasn't letting the band swing enough. So they opted for a small group together (later Shorty Rogers' Giants), separate recordings with larger, more unusual combinations and Shelly opened a drum school. First of all though, while the gathering of like-minded musicians proceeded, they worked in bassist Howard Rumsey's group at The Lighthouse, on Hermosa Beach.

White West Coast jazz for the remainder of the 1950s was to be closely identified with the outcome of these early projects; with the sound and style of Rogers's writing and the skill and precision of Manne's drumming. The former became synonymous with up-tempo, essentially 'happy'-sounding themes, generally made with short, repetitive, on-the-beat phrases, then for a clean, spirited and often European-based development of these via the orchestration. Complementing this, Shelly Manne insisted that a drummer's foremost task was to swing the rhythm section. But he added that finesse and control were also important, and that a drummer should be versatile — able to colour his beat with a wide variety of effects and augmenting his kit with extra cymbals, timpani-mallets and the like. It all made for jazz which was highly-organised, uncomplicatedly rhythmic, extremely accomplished, but still open to discoveries of form, and new improvisational content. A number of fine soloists then went into orbit with Rogers and Manne, notably Art Pepper, alto-saxophone, Bud Shank, alto-saxophone and flute, Bob Cooper, tenor-saxophone and oboe, Hampton Hawes and Claude Williamson playing piano, and Curtis Counce (bass).

Mulligan's last work before quitting New York consisted of the 'New Sounds' items for Prestige, with a ten-piece band which anticipated his later Capitol Tentette recordings and with, for the very first time, his name down as leader. But the dates did little to lift his depression and he hitchhiked towards the West in a slow and vague fashion. Being on the move like this was in fact no strange experience for him. Although born into a strictly orthodox Catholic family, the fourth of four sons, his father as an industrial engineer was regularly being moved, from Queens in New York to Marion, Ohio, to Chicago, Kalamazoo, Detroit, Reading and then to Philadelphia where Gerry stayed put for a longer section of his youth and where he remembers fooling around with a ukelele before his interest grew in the clarinet and saxophone family. So now he revisited Reading and spent some weeks in Albuquerque before waving 'goodbye' to his final hitch into Los Angeles.

When Gerry arrived on the Coast (this was Spring 1952) he naturally made contact with Rogers, Manne and the other modern jazz residents. He even played with them occasionally. He did a series of weekends at The Lighthouse with a borrowed horn (twelve hours on the stand every Saturday and Sunday); then he landed the Monday-night spot at The Haig (total capacity 85 drinkers plus bar-staff and the band) on Wilshire Boulevard run by John Bennett. Musicians who played with him there included Ernie Royal, Jimmy Rowles, Red Mitchell, and, for the first time, drummer Chico Hamilton.

He started doing freelance arranging, of which the best-remembered is his *Young Blood* score for Stan Kenton. By this time Kenton's 'Innovations In Modern Music' orchestra was dead. It had been cold and pretentious and a noticeable sterility had grown up within the music. ('Arrogance and boredom are the two most authentic products of Hell.' *André Gide*) In jazz terms Duke Ellington's adage 'It don't mean a thing if it ain't got that swing' had proved true yet again. While Quincy Jones was rather more acid: 'There has been a tendency of late to stress classical airs in many jazz works. In doing this, a lot of musicians have missed the message altogether. In short, when we stop swinging, we're competing with Ravel, Bartók, Stravinsky and a lot of other brilliant musicians on their own ground . . . musicians who easily outdo us there. Jazz must develop its own language.'

Anyway, as 1952 developed Kenton's thickets of verbiage about 'progressive jazz' had been stripped away and he was leading a conventional big band, packed with second-generation modernists. Which in turn led to his making the best LP recording of his career. 'New Concepts Of Artistry In Rhythm' is in fact the *older* concept, meaning a strong jazz propulsion. The arrangers are Bill Russo (*23 Degrees North — 82 Degrees West*, in other words '*Havana*', *Portrait Of A Count*, featuring trumpeter Conte Candoli, and *My Lady* featuring Lee Konitz); Bill Holman *(Invention For Guitar And Trumpet);* and most flowing and swinging of all, Mulligan with *Young Blood*. Stan Levey, the drummer here, is a graduate from Parker and Gillespie small groups — and Gerry's score allows him to provide a thrust and a drive which are untypical of earlier Kenton but have a therapeutic value of their own.

Gerry the arranger quickly made an impact on other West Coast musicians. I can remember in 1954 in Paris making the *faux pas* of congratulating him on 'his score' for the Kenton band of *Fascinatin' Rhythm*. 'I didn't write that,' he said, pausing over an admirer's autograph-book. 'I think you'll find in fact it was done for Stan by Bill Russo.' Nevertheless, and playing it through again, this accomplished score — especially in the flow of the saxophone section — still reminds me of the Mulligan style of big band writing. (His other scores for Kenton were *Swing House*, and early versions of *Walkin' Shoes* and *Bweebida Bobbida*.)

However: although he had certain common interests Gerry did not become a *bona fide* member of the West Coast school, and in fact today — given the benefit of hindsight — appears to stand right outside the classroom. The truth is he was about to lay the keel for Mulligan's Ark, at last. And he wanted to do things *his* way. Or rather in three ways — as soloist, composer/arranger and group leader. As a modern explorer with the baritone-saxophone his star was by now very much in the ascendant, while that of his earlier rival Serge Chaloff was fading fast. He had lightened the sound of the instrument without losing its essential richness and was playing long, supple and varied improvisations, making full use of every register,

Chet Baker.

some of which carried over into his writing, for this would become more and more linear in character — as distinct from the short, accented phrases of say, his earlier *Rocker*. Sinewy, quickly-remembered melody lines, subtly shaped by the harmonies but invariably rhythmic, came as if instinctively from his pen during these years. And they were soon to form the basic repertoire of Gerry's famous pianoless Quartet.

The concept for such a group when it first occurred to him in New York was partly because he did not like the way a favourite pianist of his, George Wallington, had been overshadowed in certain groups. 'To have an instrument with the tremendous capabilities of the piano reduced to the role of crutch for the horn solo was unthinkable.' It was, he believed, a power base in itself and therefore should remain a featured instrument. (Later on in the 1950s Gerry took to playing piano himself at concerts, usually on blues themes and in a Wallington-influenced style. But it was always as a soloist, seldom with another frontline instrument around.)

By 1952 he had realized how to do without the piano. 'The idea of a band without one is not new. The very first jazz bands did not use them; how could they? They were marching bands.' But in modern jazz, with its increased emphasis on harmonic structure? The Sidney

31

Bechet-Muggsy Spanier Big Four and the Kansas City Six of 1938/39 with Lester Young and Buck Clayton had dispensed with a piano but compensated for it with the use of a guitar. To answer this and other problems Gerry formed the Quartet with Chet Baker on trumpet, himself, Bob Whitlock on bass and Chico Hamilton on drums. Soon afterwards Carson Smith replaced Whitlock, then Larry Bunker replaced Hamilton and within two years Bob Brookmeyer had taken over from Baker, but playing a valve-trombone. Even so, it was clear from the outset what Gerry had decided on musically. He used the bass not merely as a rhythmic pivot or in alliance with the drums, but also as a third harmonic voice. (On rare occasions when he needed a fourth or fifth note in the chord he let the bass-player and/or the drummer hum them.) Immediately it produced a fresh, yet balanced and very logical ensemble. Moreover an open-sounding one, for as the line of the bass came through it became easier to hear the overall harmonic development of a performance.

'I've always worked closer with the bass than most players,' Gerry says by way of explanation. 'A lot of players *do* listen to the bass, but most guys listen more, say, to the drums. And it's quite possible a lot listen to the piano — whatever the basic set-up of your rhythm section is. But I've always been bass-orientated with everything I do, and it's the nature of the instrument. Because to me the interest of what I play consists of the intervals I can hit with the bass. Constantly shifting intervals, and we get lovely little things between ourselves.'

The other main feature of the group was the series of extended, elastic and durable lines Mulligan interwove with his frontline partner. Some of the finest written and improvised counterpoint ever played by jazz musicians.

Far from causing a mass redundancy of pianists, the Mulligan Quartet brought a new awareness that harmonic responsibility could always be shifted. Which in turn brought more freedom of action to those pianists who remained with groups. (Especially Bill Evans in the Miles Davis Sextet of 1958.)

Trumpeter Chesney 'Chet' Baker (b.1929) was a product of college and army bands. He played with a small tone and a limited range, but the contours of his lines and above all his sensitivity seemed to fit with Mulligan's concept. After he had played with Gerry at The Haig club in Los Angeles and recorded with the Quartet he was suddenly a jazz hero.

Gerry's own comments on Baker make interesting reading. 'He [Chet] was,' he says, 'the most perfect foil to work with. I've never yet to this day played with a musician who's quicker or less afraid to make a mistake. We'd sail into some song as a group . . . we'd never played it before, never discussed it — it'd sound like an arrangement. People would think it was an arrangement! You must lock it in like that and play it that same way always, they'd say. Modulations; endings — this is the wild thing. On the one hand it's so simple, making endings — and yet it can be *hard*. Because everybody's trying to avoid the cliché. Chet and I would roar into the cliché with open arms, take it, turn it around, twist it inside out, tie bows on it, and it would come out as just an ideal ending.

'Chet was a kind of fresh talent. He came along, there's no figuring where his influences were, where he learned what he knew. And his facility . . . I've never been around anybody who had a quicker relationship between his ears and his fingers. He was just uncanny — with that kind of real control; it's as simple as breathing with him. It's something that seldom happens, a talent that comes out in full bloom'.

Carson Smith (b.1931) had played with commercial bands before Gerry, but had the necessary pure tone and fine fingering to cope with all the latter's harmonic demands. Meanwhile Foreststorn 'Chico' Hamilton (b.1921) was more than just an advertisement for good black-and-white relations. He had played for six years with Lena Horne, played all the featured percussion in the film *Road To Bali* and had developed into one of the most articulate drummers in jazz; exciting, very swinging, equally adept with sticks or brushes and (most important from Gerry's point of view) a master of dynamics. Finally Bob Brookmeyer (b.1929) from Kansas City. He too had played with Claude Thornhill (on second piano and tenor-trombone), and had done a month with Woody Herman just before joining Mulligan. He is an inventive, enterprising and witty soloist on an instrument that does not come easily to jazz; and he has remained in a flexible continuing association with Gerry through to the present day. Their 1981 Japanese recordings together show no diminution in their enjoyment at swapping ideas.

This Japanese LP (Aurex EWJ-80208) is highly recommended. I recall walking into Doug Dobell's shop in London just in time to hear what is still the finest Freddie Hubbard solo I know — *Crisis* with the dynamic trumpeter backed by Roland Hanna (piano), Ray Brown (bass) and Art Blakey (drums). It happened as well to be the opening track and afterwards I said to myself: how do you follow that? But Mulligan and Brookmeyer have the confidence and talent to do so; at least this was how the record's editor felt (picking performances from three different concerts). They do a fresh-sounding *Bernie's Tune* backed by the same rhythm and then Gerry gives one of his most sensitive renderings of *Song For Strayhorn*. And naturally he is in on the final jam session number, Milt Jackson's *Bag's Groove*. He politely allows the composer to solo first — but then he is next in line, ahead of Stan Getz, Hubbard et al.

Other players would follow each other into the Quartet, especially as Gerry got into the habit of taking time off to do other projects. Jon Eardley and Art Farmer on trumpet; Red Mitchell, Bill Crow and Joe Benjamin, bass; Frank Isola and Dave Bailey on drums. Each of these made outstanding contributions to the later Quartets. But it was Baker, Hamilton and Brookmeyer we chiefly associate with the 'key' years 1952/54, the years when Gerry ended his stint at The Haig and grew to become acclaimed internationally — even by people not normally appreciative of jazz.

And all of this time themes continued to spill out of him, a majority of which are now regarded as jazz classics: *Nights At The Turntable, Gold Rush, Line For Lyons, Walkin' Shoes, Five Brothers, Limelight, Bark For Barksdale, Motel, Soft Shoe* and *Bweebida Bobbida*; while his arrangements of certain popular songs were so good that the songs themselves became almost the exclusive domain of the group — *Lullaby Of The Leaves, My Funny Valentine, Frenesi, Aren't You Glad You're You, Makin' Whoopee* and of course *Strike Up The Band* (for which he borrowed a crack from Peter Ind and called *Bike Up The Strand*). Sometimes he varied the formula for recording and added Lee Konitz to the group, giving it the extra line of counterpoint. But on these sessions Chet Baker reveals a number of deficiencies and in places fumbles badly. Nowadays we tend to value the titles with Konitz more for Lee's own superb solos. The altoist had been pining somewhat within the confines of the Kenton band and eagerly grasped at the opportunity to return to small-group jazz. His playing on *Too Marvellous For Words, I Can't Believe That You're In Love With me* and, most especially, on *Lover Man* is some of the most fertile of his entire career.

More satisfying for Mulligan contributions is the Tentette LP of 1953 for Capitol. Gerry and Chet take the main solos. And importantly it gave Gerry a chance to write within a larger format again — and perhaps the taste to lead such a group on a regular basis.

'When we were first playing at The Haig with the Quartet,' Gerry recalls, 'I started the Tentette as a rehearsal band to have something to write for. It was . . . essentially my own quartet with Chet combined with the ensemble instrumentation of the Miles Davis nonet. Musically I think the ensemble worked perfectly with the quartet concept and the band was very easy to write for. I would like to have pursued it further at that time, but *c'est la vie.*'

For the Capitol sessions he used two trumpets, valve-trombone, French horn, tuba, alto-saxophone, two baritone-saxophones, bass and drums. He re-scored *Rocker* (leaving out the thematic variation he had written for the Miles Davis session but thickening up the backdrops to the solos) and he largely reconstructed Wallington's *Godchild* under the title of *Ontet*. *A Ballad* reflects the Gil Evans affinities and also harks back to another ballad, *Darn That Dream*, once penned featuring vocalist Kenny Hagood with the Davis band; while *Flash, Westwood Walk* and *Takin' A Chance On Love* all give evidence of his sureness now as a composer and/or arranger. Also his directness. He likes to quote Dizzy Gillespie on this last subject. 'His writing imperative is, it's not what you put in, it's what you leave out. My aim is . . . to avoid undue complication. The function of the arranger is to set up a framework for the players to express themselves . . . and not only the soloists but the whole ensemble. I want things to arrive as naturally as possible.'

In the meantime though there was the question of the Quartet's success. For the world would demand that this remain Mulligan's essential outlet for years to come. Max Harrison has suggested more than one reason why its reception was so swift and, at the same time, so widespread. 'Firstly,' he writes, 'the group's outward modernity accorded well with the view widely expressed in the bulk of American jazz writing that newness is intrinsically good. Along with the prestige this entailed was the actual simplicity of the music. We have seen that its instrumentation threw emphasis on clear melodic expression and simple rhythmic construction. The resulting lack of tension was another attraction. Whereas artists like Tatum and

Parker compel our attention with the hectic complexity of their work, the somewhat detached relaxation of the Mulligan Quartet entertains and even intrigues the listener without unduly involving him. Thus, audiences who failed to respond to the uncompromising attitude of be-bop or the Davis 1948/49 band were able, in listening to the Quartet, to congratulate themselves on their advanced taste while really experiencing quite straightforward music. Other factors were the presence in the repertoire of many familiar melodies like *Lady Is A Tramp* and *Moonlight In Vermont* to which a new piquancy was given by the 'different' treatments. The air of rather smart disillusionment that surrounds interpretations like *My Funny Valentine* [a Chet Baker solo feature: R.H.] would also be sympathetic to superficially sophisticated audiences.'

Since I compiled and partly wrote the book in which this particular view is expressed (1), obviously I considered it had some foundation. And to a degree I still do, certainly the part about those audiences to whom fashion and being thought fashionable are more important than the music and its quality. On the other hand, true simplicity in art is often quite deliberate and has to be worked for very hard (for example Georges Braque, much of Picasso and of course in the cutouts of the dying Matisse). While in Mulligan's case the 'simplicity' occurred as the result of his phasing out what he considered to be inessential. I think of greater significance though — and again taking advantage of hindsight: if the music of the Quartet had been basically shallow then it would not have lasted as strongly as it has, with re-releases of the early records still selling well and an almost annual revival of the Quartet for concerts. And I put this down to three things: the instantly recognisable sound of the group; the inherent quality of Gerry's own baritone solos; and the quality and memorable nature of his composed themes and subsequent improvisations with Baker and others.

One other, equally important feature of the Quartet's success was its being able to make good records (on the Pacific Jazz and Fantasy labels). The group was always well-recorded, always well-presented and publicised, and their 78 rpm singles and early 10-inch LPs then leased to other jazz labels all around the globe. ('We were getting tremendous airplay on all kinds of stations. Like, here's poor old isolated jazz getting plays on pop programmes!' *Mulligan.)*

(1) 'Jazzmen Of Our Time, ed. R. Horricks, Victor Gollancz, London 1959.

Richard Bock of the fledgling Pacific Jazz label was the producer behind most of the record success. 'The Quartet's recording history had its beginnings on the afternoon of 10 June 1952,' he remembers, 'in Los Angeles recording engineer Philip Turetsky's tiny Laurel Canyon bungalow in the Hollywood Hills. Gerry asked Jimmy Rowles, Red Mitchell and Chico Hamilton to meet up at Turetsky's home where I had access to his Ampex tape-recorder and one RCA 44-b microphone. For some reason Rowles failed to arrive so we decided to record anyway — without a piano.

'A week later, at the Monday-night session at The Haig, Mulligan and Chet Baker met.' Jazz history was about to be made. 'After five Monday nights,' Bock continues, 'Gerry felt the Quartet was ready to record. On the afternoon of 16 August 1952, at the Turetsky's bungalow again, we recorded the memorable *Bernie's Tune* and *Lullaby Of The Leaves*. That record, released as a single in the fall of 1952 put Pacific Jazz in business. The Quartet rapidly became a West Coast sensation.' At The Haig Gerry's salary was increased to 200 dollars a week, and when his group travelled to San Francisco to play at The Blackhawk, Dave Brubeck arranged some further recordings for the Fantasy label. Otherwise Gerry remained loyal to Bock for the period before he left California to tour more widely.

What Bock refers to as 'inevitable changes and growing pains' saw Chico Hamilton lured back to Lena Horne's accompanying group for much more money. And when, shortly after the dates with Lee Konitz, 'Gerry ran foul of the narcotics law and spent six months at the Sheriff's Honor Farm', he returned to find that Chet Baker had formed his own quartet — with Russ Freeman on piano.

Mulligan accuses outside business interests of inducing Chet Baker to quit the Quartet and form his own group. But he pays tribute to Bob Brookmeyer for coming in and tackling an especially difficult role. 'I'd known him years before when I had the group with Kai [Winding], Wallington and Red Rodney. We'd been playing in Kansas City, and he [Bob] was a very young trombone-player who used to sit in with us. A beautiful player and a really lovely person. At the point when we had the Quartet going, with Chet, Chico and Bob Whitlock at The Haig, for a month or so only a couple of blocks away Stan Getz came in with the group that he had with Brookmeyer. Stan loved the sound of our Quartet, and they had adopted that kind of approach to what they were doing. So when I realised Chet had become a bandleader on his own I called Bobby and asked him to take over. We discussed the problem, you know, of a trombone replacing a trumpet — which was never intended to be the situation. Ideally, if we'd had our preferences, what we would have had was Chet *and* Bobby and me, because the three of us could have done the three-horn frontline with the same kind of contrapuntal ease. Bobby and I never had it that easy, because he was always stuck into that role of being a substitute trumpet-player trying to play lines against himself.

'These are the kinds of thing there's no reason for people to be aware of, I suppose. But that strain always hampered Bobby with the group, and it was something we were always conscious of as well. We tried to do everything we could to alleviate it, but the only *real* solution would have been to have the trumpet with us.' (Hence Jon Eardley and later Art Farmer.)

Already Mulligan had used Lee Konitz as a guest soloist with the Quartet on records. Next, towards the end of 1954 he featured Zoot Sims and Bob Brookmeyer with it at a West Coast concert (Jon Eardley was in playing trumpet by this date). He was so pleased with the effect that he decided to keep it going and this Sextet toured Europe in 1955 and recorded the outstanding 'Mainstream' LP of the following year. But Mulligan maintains the group was never at its best in the studios. 'Live, we'd have that presence, that big, spread-out sound of many instruments, when it was just four horns really. By the end of the night we'd wind up with the horns spread across the stage. Jon Eardley would be over there, Zoot would be there, Bob here and I'd be right here — like, ninety feet apart. And it's a presence of sound, you see. It happened so naturally, because we'd start out . . . and as we went along, the whole thing opened up.' Longtime Mulligan watcher and collector Gordon Jack, who has equipped me with various recorded items, including an exciting 'live' version of Gerry's *Broadway* by the Sextet, sums it up in his own way. 'It has always seemed to me,' he says, 'that very few jazz groups of the '50s paid much attention to an ensemble *style* — being more concerned with long solos, while the other horns went outside for a smoke. Well, the Mulligan Sextet could never be accused of this . . .'

Drummer Dave Bailey has this to say of the Sextet: 'It was *extremely* musical and it was a music education for me. It was the first time I was exposed to music with the subtleties Gerry required. It also

Lee Konitz.

helped greatly that I was able to read music because I was able to utilise it. If anything stands out, it was the impact of the Sextet when the Sextet was on its game. It was a dynamic band that could sound like a much larger band and do very subtle things.' However, as Bill Crow, who replaced Peck Morrison on bass points out: 'It was not all sweetness and light. We took a bus to Paris . . . and they put us on as one of the vaudeville turns at the Olympia Theatre. We were just one of the many acts. I think they opened with the trained seals and the jugglers and the comics. And then we came out as the American jazz band, the next to the closing of the first half of the programme. The closing was the Nicholas Brothers. And the headliner that closed the second half was Jacqueline François. So there were very few jazz fans in the audience and a lot of them just looked at us. It was really funny.'

Some of the potency of Gerry's musical thinking was also carried over into the 'Jazz Concerto Grosso' LP of 1957 made with Brookmeyer and cornetist Phil Sunkel as the rest of the frontline. This LP is now hard to come by, but is an excellent example of how Mulligan, an archetypal weaver of horizontal lines can, in good company, keep the invention going until only the dictates of groove and time force him to call a halt.

Even so, by mid-1958 and now back in New York, Gerry was rehearsing another Quartet, with Art Farmer, Bill Crow and Dave Bailey.

Another English musician — and another baritone-player — spent a lot of his time in Mulligan's company while their later rehearsals were going on. Ronnie Ross (who the following year would win the *Down Beat* 'New Star' award) was in the United States as a member of the Newport International Band directed by Marshall Brown. Gerry — although increasingly critical of the way 'big business' Newport was now being run — appeared there that year to play a special duet with Harry Carney and the Ellington band (*Prima Bara Dubla*). Duke did not even tell the two he had written the piece until the afternoon before the concert. Carney and Gerry thought they would just be jamming on *Perdido* or something!

Mulligan immediately befriended Ross and, as the latter says, was extremely kind and helpful. 'There was no side with him, and certainly no jealousy because I played the same instrument. In fact once at a party we accidentally grabbed each other's baritones — and it was a strangely thrilling experience to hear the things he played so well coming through my horn. He often took me along to rehearsals, where Art [Farmer] and the others were able to work from published parts: the Mulligan compositions had become so popular by this time. He also took me to The Black Pearl, a nightclub where they looked you over through a spy-hole before opening the door, to hear Lester Young.

'I asked Gerry how he got his sound across when playing in front of really powerhouse drummers like Max Roach or Art Blakey. "It's a matter of concentrating your sound," he said. "If you just try to blow louder then you ruin your tone. But with will-power you can concentrate the sound, giving it the kind of intensity needed to play very directly at an audience." Another thing, although he loved jam sessions, by the time I got to know him he wouldn't generally take part at one *after* a concert. And he didn't like his sidemen playing at them either. He said they should have given so much of themselves at the performance that night they'd be exhausted and didn't need to go on and play again.'

Ronnie concludes: 'Because earlier players had used a rich, fruity tone on the baritone, when they came to play fast numbers they tended to sound as if a bumble-bee had got loose. But Mulligan's purity of sound and agile fingering changed all that. Which leads me to another fascinating thing he does. Apart from the supporting sling around one's neck there is a little hook on the baritone to hold its weight up with the right-hand thumb. Well, don't ask me how he manages it, but Gerry ignores the hook and so is able to add his thumb to the right-hand fingering. I can usually get around the instrument pretty fast, and yet I've never succeeded in doing without the thumbhold. Gerry can make a side B flat and a top E playing this way. However, there you are: if you're so much of a virtuoso then it becomes possible to rewrite the rule-book as you go along!

'Incidentally too the baritone he plays is an old crossbar Conn. It's at least fifty years old. And he uses a Gale mouthpiece made in Los Angeles — the only jazzman I know who does. I tried one but it didn't give me the right sound. In jazz you have to keep trying until you find what's right for you, for *your* expression.'

Chapter Four

An Ark suggests a vessel that is unusually crowded; and some willed concentration of detail on my own part becomes necessary at this stage. For if as intended I devote the last section of my profile to the enlarged ship that is Mulligan's Orchestra, or as it is sometimes called his Concert Band, then first I must mention as many as possible of the musical exploits which have happened all around its existence. They are the interlinear going with his main career as a bandleader, but no less interesting for being fragmentary. For the man has been ubiquitous. As the 1960s *Encyclopedia Of Jazz* states: 'He has retained a casual pleasure in playing in any context and has frequently appeared at jazz festivals during the '60s working with Dixieland, Swing and be-bop groups, sitting in with big bands, and generally showing a lust for playing and a rare enthusiasm and communication with his audiences.' 'With Gerry,' Dave Brubeck adds, 'you feel as if you're listening to the past, present and future of jazz all the time, and it's with such taste and respect that you're not quite aware of the changes in idiom. Mulligan gets the old New Orleans two-beat going with a harmonic awareness of advanced jazz, and you feel not that tradition is being broken, but rather that it's being pushed forward.'

From the late 1950s he sat in whenever and wherever he could, toured extensively (including Europe and Japan) and at one stage (1966) experimented with a rather unsatisfactory group involving baritone, guitar and rhythm. Again in 1966 he collaborated with Bill Holman on a longer work, *Music For Baritone-Saxophone And Orchestra*, which he introduced as its featured soloist with the Los Angeles Neophonic Orchestra. (No commercial record of this exists.)

He also continued the practice of recording with other major figures. In 1957 alone he made more LPs than a lot of 'name' jazzmen can boast in a lifetime. I can only discuss a few I judge to be truly outstanding. (Otherwise, thank God for my discographer!)

It began with the unlikely 'Mulligan Meets Monk' LP for Riverside. Perhaps not so unlikely though, because by this time Gerry and Thelonious had become firm friends. It went back to that same 1954 Paris jam session I referred to earlier as beginning — to borrow the title of Gerry's own signature-tune — in *Utter Chaos*. Monk whipped out some of his most advanced and previously unheard harmonies, and immediately there were anxious frowns from the other musicians. But Gerry then rallied and the set only ended (abruptly) when Mrs Mulligan reappeared. Yet, it was an important set in that it left the two composers filled with curiosity about each other's music.

Danny Halperin tells how the next day Thelonious was thoroughly depressed about the way European audiences were reacting to his music. 'They're not really listening to what I'm playing,' he complained. Mulligan overheard this and turned to the pianist. 'Don't bother about it,' he said quickly. '*I'll* be listening to you from now on. I'll be just off-stage listening. If you turn a little that way you'll see me there.' And Thelonious played his next concert like that, with his imposing figure slightly averted from the piano and turned towards the wings. It marked the beginning of a creative understanding between the two men.

They agreed that for the Riverside sessions they would use the rhythm section from Monk's Quartet at The Five Spot in New York. Mulligan had worked with ex-Count Basie drummer Shadow Wilson previously, but Wilbur Ware on bass was a new experience for him and he expressed delight at the latter's unusually melodic and imaginative playing. He himself partly determined the instrumentation though. Producer Orrin Keepnews had intended to do only one session with a quartet. For the second he wanted to build the two composer/soloists into a larger band. However, after the first evening (when *I Mean You*, *Rhythm-A-Ning* and *Straight, No Chaser* were recorded) Gerry insisted that they complete the album with exactly the same musicians. He particularly wanted, he explained, to explore

43

the modern jazz classic *'Round About Midnight* with its composer and without any other soloists coming between them. And he got his way. Keepnews comments: 'The atmosphere on both occasions was one of complete and fruitful relaxation. There was too much mutual respect and affection on hand for there to be any danger of feelings of competitiveness getting in the way.'

Mulligan's exploration of *'Round About Midnight* is a two-part affair, first of its uniquely sinister mood, then as Wilson and Ware impose a subtle swing of the theme's internal technicalities. Gerry himself introduced only one of his own compositions to the session, the up-tempo *Decidedly* based on the chords of Charlie Shavers' *Undecided.*

After this his appetite had been whetted no matter how diverse the other performers. In the years which followed he embarked upon albums with Johnny Hodges, Stan Getz, Ben Webster, blues singer Jimmy Witherspoon and late in 1977 Lionel Hampton, to name but a few.

Again dating back to 1957 there is a particularly satisfying LP with the late Paul Desmond on alto-saxophone, another expert inventor of long, contrapuntal lines.

The gestation of this Mulligan-Desmond collaboration ('Blues In Time') began — like the Monk one — in 1954. Gerry sat in with the Dave Brubeck Quartet at a Carnegie Hall concert and a *Tea For Two* resulted which convinced both saxophone players that their ways of making music had, in Gerry's words, 'a natural affinity'. Nothing more happened then during the three years before August 1957 because Desmond was under contract to one record label and GM favoured certain others. Until Norman Granz took a hand and offered to swap an artist from his stable to Desmond's company for an LP if Paul was released to do the album with Mulligan. So, the date duly took place and, apart from Gerry's own fine playing, is — in this writer's opinion — the best record of Paul Desmond's entire output. He was always a seemingly effortless inventor of improvised ideas, but Gerry's presence has clearly inspired him to take a number of daring chances, both tonally and with harmonics, which I do not believe he ever did with anyone else on record. 'I'm very proud of several things we did on the date,' the severely self-critical Mulligan stated afterwards. 'Like sometimes we're blowing passages in thirds, and they come off. It's a little alarming. And there are also the places where Paul comes through so strongly, much more

Bob Brookmeyer, Bill Crow, Dave Bailey and Gerry Mulligan

aggressively than he usually plays with Dave. He gets to swing pretty hard at times here in contrast to his more flowing and lyrical work.'

The LP is once more pianoless, the interweaving of the saxophones superb and both men contribute compositions of their own: Desmond with the title-number and *Wintersong*, Gerry with *Stand Still* and *Fall Out* and his familiar *Line For Lyons*. But another impressive feature of the album's programme of music is the ultra-slow rendition of *Body And Soul*. Although this is still the much-played 32-bar standard by Johnny Green, both GM and Paul play it as if they are a couple of blues singers, pulling out the kind of 'soul searching' we normally associate with Billie Holiday or the great Ray Charles. And, of course, it hints at why Gerry could later make such a good record with Jimmy Witherspoon.

A later collaboration between Mulligan and Desmond entitled 'Two Of A Mind' is not quite so evenly fine as 'Blues In Time' but includes a genuinely outstanding track based on *Out Of Nowhere*, one of the best bright-tempoed duets Gerry has played with *any* other musician. In unfortunate contrast, the full potential and promising beginning of the sessions with Stan Getz was marred by their deciding (or being persuaded) to swap instruments for the second side of the LP and then each sounding distinctly uncomfortable with an alien horn.

Different again, but this time in fascinating contrast with the Desmond recordings, since it involves Gerry with another of the legendary alto-saxophones of jazz, is the 1960 LP with Johnny Hodges. And also this time a pianist is involved in the person of Claude Williamson, an excellent technician and soloist who had been a West Coast resident from long before GM's move there. In the course of the LP, 'Gerry Mulligan Meets Johnny Hodges', he inserts a marvellously sensitive solo passage, for instance, during *What's The Rush*, which is in turn an instrumental version of one of the songs Gerry had been co-writing with Judy Holliday. But let us concentrate here on the subject of Mulligan and Hodges, because whereas the recordings with Desmond had achieved inventive excitement, the album with Hodges offers an example of jazz created from unadulterated sensual beauty. Which, in effect, was Hodges' musical trademark.

To anyone who ever travelled with the Duke Ellington Orchestra, Hodges, alias 'The Rabbit', could come across as a very prickly character indeed. It was largely, I then judged, a question of ego and a personal envy of his leader — and I have commented on his neglect of the rest of the Duke's saxophones elsewhere (2). On the other hand, once it became a matter of playing solos, especially on records — and with ego still to the fore — he could be relied upon to blow like an absolute angel. He was (and remains on his LPs) one of the supreme alto-saxophone stylists of jazz music. By comparison with his peers (Benny Carter, Charlie Parker, Lee Konitz, Paul Desmond and Eric Dolphy) he would improvise amazingly few notes, but then project them with a poise, a romantic and languid line and, above all, a satiny tone which made Mulligan, among many young players, a consistent admirer.

Gerry already had a much-praised LP with another former Ellingtonian (Ben Webster) under his belt and was as keen to do something with Hodges as he had with Paul Desmond and just before that

(2) To Derek Jewell for his biography of Duke Ellington, Sphere Books, London 1978.

Monk. 'Johnny,' he said [to Nat Hentoff], 'has been one of the men I most enjoyed hearing as long as I can remember. I started playing alto in my teens, after clarinet, and became particularly interested in Hodges's work with the Ellington band.' And he hit out at certain critics who were knocking the work of these older jazzmen. 'The compulsion to say something "new" every day is a significantly immature way of looking at life. The constant drive to force musicians and other artists to constantly invent something "new" is one of the banes of the creative life; and this particular kind of pressure, incidentally, also reveals something of our whole culture. In any case, if there are people who cannot hear how thoroughly mature and individual Hodges is, I'm sorry for them.'

Norman Granz flew Hodges to Los Angeles for the recordings. Meanwhile Gerry had been preparing three of his compositions for the sessions, *What's The Rush* and two brand-new ones, *Bunny* and *18 Carrots For Rabbit*. He himself plays with what I prefer to think of as dutiful sincerity on the album. He shows his immense respect for Hodges by letting the overall sound be like that of the typical Ellington small groups of the 1940s — and as a result the senior soloist is at his most composed and rewarding. *What's The Rush* would have been a credit to one of the Duke's own recording sessions; while Hodges's own notable slow ballad in turn features Gerry at his most perceptive and sonorous (*Shady Side*). Only *18 Carrots For Rabbit* breaks the pattern, having a more boppish line and chord sequence. But Hodges is plainly enjoying himself by this time and drummer Mel Lewis then trades passages with Mulligan and Williamson.

A further affirmation of jazz roots was bound to occur when Gerry agreed to play the 'live' shows (and resulting LP) with Jimmy Witherspoon which took place at the Renaissance Club in Los Angeles on 2 and 9 December 1959: in fact just as plans were being worked out for the collaboration with Johnny Hodges.

This is very much a Witherspoon outing, characterised by his earthy, swinging and totally urban interpretation of the kind of blues first pioneered by Jimmy Rushing and 'Big' Joe Turner in the 1930s. But to back Spoon's individual updating of their work we have in attendance Gerry, the formidable Ben Webster, Jimmy Rowles on piano, Leroy Vinnegar (bass) and Mel Lewis again on drums. Obviously the themes had to be chosen to feature the singer, ranging from Ma Rainey's *C.C.Rider* and Leroy Carr's *How Long* to

W.C.Handy's *St.Louis Blues* and the well-known, but still composer-untraced *Outskirts Of Town*. However, it does need to be added that Gerry seems to have the capacity to turn other jazz people on, whether they be Paul Desmond, Johnny Hodges or, as in this case, Witherspoon, Webster and the rhythm section. As a longstanding collector of Spoon's records the one under discussion here has definitely become my favourite. And the baritone solos, obbligatos and general pieces of accompaniment are no small part of the play. Ben Webster too makes good contributions, reminding us that he was the one musician on the dates who played these same blues behind Rushing and Joe Turner in the famed Kansas City clubs.

The only technical flaw on this particular LP (issued from Milan, Italy by Servizio Joker) is an abrupt editing into the audience applause at the ends of certain tracks. Mechanical fades on the remixed master tape would have sounded much cleaner.

Finally among these reviews, I will briefly touch on the Gate LP with Lionel Hampton. With an artist of Mulligan's calibre it is not difficult to find good things to say about his talent or his main innovations. Where the problem arises is that, given his all-embracing view of jazz and his being musically footloose anyway, how does one keep pace with every area into which he ventures? So I will confess to having an ongoing weakness for the album with Hamp; yes, even though it has its obvious blemishes, apparently as the result of some bad organisation and Lionel having to double between performing (albeit not on every track) and his other function as the record's producer. For all that it is a very swinging set, with much interpolated wit by both Gerry and the vibes virtuoso. Moreover it contains one masterly Mulligan ballad solo with an equally sincere one by Hampton during the *Song For Johnny Hodges* track. Gerry has managed to give a soaring, lyrical impression of 'The Rabbit' in his composed lines; while Hamp is clearly remembering with emotion his great 1937 recording with Hodges of *On The Sunny Side Of The Street*. Otherwise this is an LP devoted to fun and happiness; and jazz music has a requirement for these as well. As Art Blakey put it, 'If I'm playing and I don't see people tapping their feet and having themselves a ball, that's when I get worried . . .' (3).

---

(3) Also Alun Morgan points out in his sleeve-notes the cleverness of Gerry's theme *Blight Of The Fumble Bee:* a 12-bar blues wherein the soloists have the option of playing different chords over bars 9 to 12.

Johnny Hodges.

Standing somewhat apart from the various Mulligan collaborations with other jazz luminaries, though also superb, are two albums made in the GM vintage year of 1964 with another Sextet: 'Butterfly With Hiccups' and 'Night Lights'. The presence of Brookmeyer and trumpet and flugelhorn specialist Art Farmer with Gerry here suggests at first perusal a recreation of the travelling Sextet of the mid-1950s, but in fact this isn't so. Zoot Sims has been replaced not by another tenor-saxophone but with Jim Hall on guitar; and the resulting records are a studio concept to make outstanding jazz with good and sympathetic partners.

I stress this last point because, in a long recording career, it is not always possible (or indeed necessary) to approach every single session as being of vital importance to the developing history of jazz. The criterion is first and foremost to make music which is intrinsically fine. As I have been writing in the book thus far, other exploits by Gerry Mulligan have been influential to jazz: his work with Elliot Lawrence, Miles/Gil Evans, *Young Blood* for Stan Kenton, then his own Quartets, and Sextet, plus his continuing big band, of which more later. These are the major events of the essential Mulligan canon — and which, if he had achieved nothing else, would still guarantee his lasting position in jazz. But alongside them are the remaining creative efforts, like the sessions with Desmond, Hodges et al; and we can enjoy these simply for being what they are: unique one-offs. The Sextet sessions of 1964 belong in the same category. They intersperse new themes with old GM standards like *Line for Lyons* and with other, 'classic' standards by Cole Porter, Harold Arlen, etc: *You'd Be So Nice To Come Home To, Old Devil Moon, In The Wee Small Hours*. Together with one real classic, a jazz investigation of Chopin's *Prelude in E Minor*. Above all though they portray consumate musicianship. Brookmeyer by this date had fully matured as a soloist while Art Farmer has seldom played better on record. Jim Hall reaffirms his standing as the most delicately exciting of jazz guitarists. And Gerry (often switching to piano) is both an inspiring general and the ultimate enricher of the two sessions. So, definitely not to be missed.

Chapter Five

From 1968 Mulligan began to undertake a series of tours with the Dave Brubeck Quartet. Paul Desmond had finally left it in 1967 to begin writing a book called *How Many Of You Are There In The Quartet?*. Gerry was later reported as having played in 'an unusually gutsy manner' while with Brubeck. And of becoming a self-indulgent piano-player. 'I've enjoyed playing with Dave very much,' he remarked of this time. 'We do have a certain affinity . . . if I'm working with a piano, then of course that's the colour of the group, and that's what we adapt to. It's kind of a funny thing, but . . . not only have I subbed for Paul Desmond, but one night when Dave had a concert at Carnegie (Hall), *Dave* fell sick and he asked me to substitute for him on piano. Well, as a pianist . . . I'm subject to moods. Some nights I just play as if I can do no wrong. Other times I feel like I'm struggling. But I still enjoy it all. So this was one of those nights when everything came off right for me. Great. And it's fun. Since then Dave and I have taken turns in trying to wipe each other out!'

He was also in full flight as a composer again and his themes going into the 1970s are just as memorable, but if anything more intriguingly subtle than those of the 1950s for the Quartet. *For An Unfinished Woman* and *Song For Strayhorn* are outstanding by any melodic standards; but the others are all of high quality — *Golden Notebooks, Maytag, 42nd And Broadway, K-4 Pacific, Country Beaver, Walk On The Water, It's Sandy At The Beach, Grand Tour, A Weed In Disneyland* and *By Your Grace*.

In 1971 he recorded with a big new ensemble he called 'The Age

Of Steam' for the A & M label and appeared with the same format at the Newport Jazz Festival/New York.

Among Mulligan's various larger group albums 'The Age Of Steam' LP is perhaps the odd one out; but no less enjoyable or interesting for being just that. It is in addition almost entirely concerned with movement of some sort, whether it's *K-4 Pacific*, named after a Pennsylvania R.R. locomotive which once ran past Gerry's Ohio house, or *Maytag* which recalls the chug and bumping of his mother's washing-machine. *Over The Hill And Out Of The Woods* is about human movement; then there is animal movement (with *Country Beaver*) and the movement of a man stealing things from a woman (*Golden Notebooks*, inspired by Doris Lessing's novel of the same title). Even the quiet and stunningly beautiful *Grand Tour* has its own inbuilt hymnal and formal forward progression.

Gerry had opted for an unusually large rhythm section which naturally reinforces these impressions of movement. And good solos abound — by the fleet-fingered Howard Roberts on guitar (on *A Weed In Disneyland*), Brookmeyer again, Tom Scott (tenor and soprano-saxes), Bud Shank (alto-saxophone and flute) — plus ex-Basieite Harry 'Sweets' Edison on trumpet. ('It was really a thrill to hear him solo on my music.' *Mulligan*) Gerry himself is fairly active on piano. Otherwise the pianist is the gifted Roger Kellaway.

Compositionally it was Gerry's first radical new departure for several years and he chose to be both more autobiographical and deliberately evocative. Plus, of course, his normal fastidious self. For he is one of that certain breed: a genuinely original, excitingly creative person who takes time after the initial creativity then to perfect what he has first of all conceived. To put it in simpler terms, you just don't hear 'bum' notes on Mulligan records. (But in common with other of his records, you do hear him throw wittily improvised baritone phrases against his own composed and arranged scores.)

Of the 'Age Of Steam' group, he had this to say: 'The main difference is the size of the rhythm section. I'd never worked with such a large section including drums and two percussionists before. They are an entire ensemble unto themselves. The trick is to make everything relate, to make all of the elements into one whole. And . . . I see this new album primarily as a vehicle for new material. During its production, there were quite a few concepts floating around.' He is no doubt referring to his childhood memories of the old Midwestern bands — and to other early pictures which he always connects with sounds. Of *K-4 Pacific*, for instance, he explains, 'I was fascinated by trains as a kid. The sound of that locomotive made a large impression on me. So I wrote this jazz chart with its sound and feeling in mind.' His earlier reference to trumpeter Harry Edison is in connection with his spirited playing on *Over The Hill And Out Of The Woods*, perhaps the most impressive and certainly surprising new piece of music on the album. One has become used to Gerry's originals being powerful melodically and very thoroughly integrated in their harmonies and construction. But here he has placed his abilities as a melodist in an episodic form. There are three quite distinctive and separate parts, and the work — including the Edison solo — lasts for almost nine minutes. Gerry is again active on piano as well as with his baritone, and afterwards announced himself happy with the scenic aspects and overall emotion of the performance.

In reality, the years immediately before his 'Age Of Steam' project had been for GM one of his rare fallow periods as regards recording. He'd continued to work with Dave Brubeck and got in on a 'pop' album with Beaver and Krauze and another, 'live' one alongside Charles Mingus. (Also too there is the illegal tape of Duke Ellington's 1969 Birthday Concert at the White House introduced by President R.M.Nixon. *See Appendix 1*) Otherwise though, as he put it to Michael Cuscuna, he was 'bored by the trendiness of much modern music' and the resulting hassles of business. Consequently when he gained the opportunity to put together 'The Age Of Steam' band he jumped at the idea. But he was then forced to reduce this to a small group to play an engagement at The Half Note in New York City.

In 1974 there occurred a successful reunion with Chet Baker, with a follow-up the next year and LPs drawn from both performances (at Carnegie Hall) on CTI. He also toured Italy and France, and spent some months as artist-in-residence at the University of Miami. Meanwhile too there were inevitably the festivals: NJF/NY, Monterey, Montreux, Nice; plus MIDEM, the annual winter shin-dig at Cannes, where publishers do their 'sincere' best to flog songs and everyone else stands around and enjoys expense-account booze.

As regards the CTI Carnegie Hall records with Chet Baker (under whose contract with producer Creed Taylor they were actually made), there are the expected reworkings of former GM Quartet items like *Line For Lyons* and Chet plays, no doubt for the several

Gerry Mulligan, Alan Dawson, Dave Brubeck and Jack Six at the Yankee Stadium, New York, 1972. Photo: David Redfern

thousandth time, his much-praised *My Funny Valentine* solo. But in addition Volume 1 contains an earlier, and somewhat quicker version of the Mulligan composition *For An Unfinished Woman,* his clearly expressed and obviously deeply-felt tribute to Judy Holliday. Chet doesn't play at all on this track, and with only vibraphone and the rhythm section behind him Gerry cannot do several of the things included on his superb big band performance of 1980. Even so, this one is still a worthwhile acquisition if only for his own improvised passages. Underpinned by the predictably fine beat of Ron Carter on bass the baritone solo ranks with his best for its mounting attack, internal architecture and, overall, its passion.

While in Italy in 1975 Gerry recorded one of his most interestingly different albums for Cream Records. It features him in the company of Giancarlo Barigozzi on flute and soprano, Enrico Intra (piano) and Sergio Farina (guitar). Enrico Intra wrote all the music except for one Mulligan bossa nova, *Rio One.* The playing is moody and at certain points soul-baring, while Gerry takes the role of partner rather than leader and on the side-long *Nuova Civilta* track contributes one of his most inventive solos on record. His technique is a model for anyone coming fresh to the baritone as an instrument. But even just sustaining notes as he does would be a difficult thing for most players. Another surprising feature is the passage played by him of what amounts to 'free' jazz. For it indicates that despite his obsession with 'roots' and/or his own highly personalised musical statements, nevertheless his ears remain widely open to other jazz developments going on around him. They take in, they sift with the brain and then they assimilate what will fit. What is played at the 'free' stage of *Nuova Civilta* offers an elasticity of notation and tone in juxtaposition with a sure grasp of form. In other words, the freedom is in the cause of invention and expression and clearly not just going on the rampage, out of control. Meanwhile *Fertile Land* on the second side of the LP is a fine ballad into which Gerry pours an acute and haunting sensitivity.

This undeservedly little known LP with Intra again reminds one how seldom it is that GM will go into a studio and record without at least one other frontline instrument present. Barigozzi plays only occasionally within the album and so the baritone is increasingly isolated towards the forward areas. We have to reach all the way back to 1963 and the 'Jeru' LP with pianist Tommy Flanagan and then to his various appearances with the Brubeck Quartet as providing suitable parallels. Yet the 'Jeru' set — with Ben Tucker on bass, Dave Bailey, drums, and here and there Alec Dorsey playing congas — affords us some of the most mature Mulligan on record as a soloist: rich in his outpouring of ideas, clear in baritone skills and with all the evident self-sufficiency of a man who has become the indisputed Number One in the world on his chosen instrument. (Would the late, gifted Bob Gordon, if he'd lived, have become a serious rival to GM? It's a neat debating point, but somehow I doubt it. Technically maybe; not for invention or sensitivity though.) Anyway, 'Jeru' offers a feast of baritone soloing, and with tracks such as Cole Porter's *Get Out Of Town*, the groovy *Blue Boy* and an ultra-relaxed *Inside Impromptu* one wonders why Gerry has been so reluctant to use the format of just one horn and rhythm. Perhaps the truth lies in the fact that he has so strong a predilection for counterpoint, and is so expert at the weaving of lines, he feels slightly uneasy about not having these aspects of jazz somewhere present.

And of course there were films, notably his playing on the soundtrack of Quincy Jones's *How To Steal A Diamond*. (Gerry's earlier appearance in *The Subterraneans* had made its own distinctive contribution to that film's permanent underground status. Nothing wrong with his playing; but Mulligan cast as a 'beat generation' preacher in sweat-shirt and crucifix, winning over a dubious, pot-smoking flock via jazz? Well, hardly . . .)

The other permanent feature to come out of the 1970s, however, has been his initial and since then increasing use of the soprano-saxophone. He first used it in public (a curved one) at the *Salute To Zoot Sims* concert of 1975. Since when, and using the normal straight-bodied variety long associated with Sidney Bechet, it has come to be a regular feature of his Orchestra.

Chapter Six

'Keep passing your life through a sieve. Go on shaking and only keep what remains, which is your essential part. Go on shaking until it becomes second nature to do so.'

— *Henri de Montherlant*
'Notebook XXII'

A mystery still surrounds what might well have been the real origination of the Mulligan Concert Band/Orchestra.

In April 1957 Gerry went into the CBS Studios with an armful of the best big band scores he had ever written. And he had on hand most of his favourite New York musicians to perform them, including, as soloists, Lee Konitz, Zoot Sims, Charlie Rouse (later Thelonious Monk's tenor-player) and Bob Brookmeyer, trumpeters Don Joseph and Jerry Lloyd (formerly Jerry Hurwitz) — Joe Benjamin on bass and Dave Bailey, or the next day Gus Johnson, on drums. Gerry had also added a second baritone, leaving himself free to play either lead or solo. Any piano passages he would take himself.

These men fully responded to the quality of the writing and interpreted the arrangements wonderfully well. As Mulligan remarked later, 'their togetherness reminded me of Ellington's trombone section of the 1930s. Lawrence Brown, Juan Tizol and Joe Nanton each had a very distinctive style, yet together they produced an amazing overall sound.' Well, there is certainly no exaggeration here. The band of April 1957 was filled with strong individual personalities but in the ensembled passages they function as one.

And this despite the writing's typical Mulligan use of often very demanding counterpoint.

And yet, for some still unexplained reason, only one title from the sessions — *Thruway* — was issued. In fact it was not until twenty years later that French pianist Henri Renaud, with the help of CBS archivist Tina McCarthy, tracked down the remainder and at last secured their release as part of the 'Gerry Mulligan, The Arranger' album. Renaud, by this time himself an executive with CBS, then enquired why they had not been issued in the first place. Only to be told, 'Oh — Gerry had rejected them as inferior'. But when he next met Mulligan the arranger vigorously denied this. 'On the contrary,' he said, 'I remember them as some of the best tracks we ever laid down.' So the mystery continues. Was it oversight; a bureaucratic slip? Or were the men with the big illegal Havanas simply going through one of their anti-jazz phases? Meanwhile the original producer George Avakian, an influential voice at CBS over this period, has kept strangely quiet about it.

However, there can be no further argument about the music itself. *All The Things You Are* is a masterpiece and one of the greatest jazz arrangements. Admittedly Gerry had chosen for his source material perhaps the finest, most original popular song of all time. But the logical skill and daring of the variations upon this song he then creates, and the integrated richness of sound he gets — these are a revelation and amount almost to a new composition. I particularly like the way, after introducing the theme himself, Gerry goes on without pause to improvise an accompanying line behind Lee Konitz. Also the ebb and flow of sound he uses to cushion the delicate trumpet-playing of Don Joseph. And again the intricacy and precision of the final chorus, where the band's phrasing and dynamics are tested to their extremes; but with purpose and confidence. As Henri Renaud says, 'the closeness of the different sections of the band, together with the blending of their respective solos, suggest a full organ with a subtle combination of stops. It makes it all the more a pity that this superb band never had a chance to function regularly.'

The other titles are all Mulligan originals, *Thruway, Motel* and *Mullenium,* and again emphasise his melodic strength as well as his taste for linear and multi-linear development. Together with, as Renaud points out, 'an indulgence in collective improvisation or 'spontaneous polyphony' reflecting his interest in traditional jazz.'

(An interest taking in Red Nichols, Bix Beiderbecke and the white Chicagoans in addition to the New Orleans masters.) Outstanding solos are included. On *Thruway* by Mulligan himself, Jerry Lloyd, Brookmeyer, Joseph, Sims and not least Lee Konitz; on *Motel* by Sims, Charlie Rouse, Brookmeyer, Mulligan and Konitz again; and on *Mullenium* by Gerry, Joseph, Brookmeyer and Sims. Which only makes their living 'burial' — like Lady Madeline's in *The Fall Of The House Of Usher* — all the more difficult to understand . . .

We now move on to 1960 when Mulligan launched an orchestra, called 'The Concert Jazz Band' on a permanent basis. This was largely made possible by impresario Norman Granz setting up the necessary tours and contracting Gerry to record for his Verve label. The newly-minted leader went for a group of thirteen players. As announced at the time, his instrumentation was decided 'because I wanted the same clarity of sound and interplay of lines that I had in the smaller groups. So, we have a clarinet in the reed section, not primarily for a clarinet-lead effect but for a sound contributing to the ensemble in general. As for the soloists, I wanted to use just a few men for the bulk of the solo work, so that they would be heard enough for the audiences to become familiar with their styles.' Obviously what he had in mind over this last point was how closely identified Lester Young had been with Count Basie; or Hodges, Carney and Cootie Williams with Duke Ellington. In other words, his sidemen became 'star' assets of the group.

There were still the familiar faces: Zoot, Bob Brookmeyer, Don Ferrara. Plus some comparatively new ones for Mulligan — Conte Candoli with the trumpets, Gene Quill, clarinet and alto-saxophone, and a different type of drummer in Mel Lewis, a man used to powering big bands. As for the band overall, its aim was to play jazz for listening, not for dancing and this remained its policy on through the 'sixties.

Peter Ind again: 'By this time I'd got an apartment in East Village, New York — with across the way (on Second Street) a big 'loft' studio (1600 square feet) I was turning into a place for recording. There were no beards in New York at this date and so the locals explained that 'a nice religious boy' had moved in. Gerry often used the studio place to rehearse in. I realized there was some personal tragedy around in his life. He'd had this longstanding relationship with the actress Judy Holliday, and, as we now know, she was suffering from an incurable cancer. Sometimes she'd come to the rehearsals, but already she looked quite ill. However, Gerry never dwelt on this in the company of the other musicians. What he felt he kept to himself. I know he's capable of very deep feeling — but he has his own self-discipline when it comes to expressing outward emotion. The real outward emotion gets through in his playing.

'As for Gerry with the musicians,' Peter Ind says, 'I could observe how success had brought in its wake a renewed sense of confidence. He'd believed in his own talent previously, but not in the way of being able to put across *all* he wanted to say. Now though he knew it was possible and consequently the earlier tension and that slight touch of bitterness had left him. He was much more at ease, and also at ease with and in control of the men who worked for him. I remember he had that leadership quality: of making the guys *want* to play well for him.'

The Concert Jazz Band recorded for Verve both in the studios and 'live' at New York's Village Vanguard. What the resulting records reveal is once more Mulligan's patience and meticulous care as a rehearser of his men. The ensemble sound is integrated, mellow and smooth-flowing. The solos are cleverly supported. And Mel Lewis's naturally fiery drumming is swinging but controlled.

A lingering criticism of this particular band's first studio recording is a certain blandness: as if the 'cool' influence has been allowed to return and dominate the earthier qualities which Gerry had worked so hard to mine over the years. The only other regret I have is its shortage of any fresh Mulligan originals. However, he partly compensates for this with some fine arrangements of popular songs — two or three of which approach the standards set by *All The Things You Are*. There is too a good concert work-out on his earlier classic theme *Bweebida Bobbida*.

What arrangements as varied as *Sweet And Slow* (with its growling blues roots and use of harmon-mutes), the Latin American-styled *Out Of This World* and another sensitive version of *My Funny Valentine* reveal is how much more his lyricism has increased over the years. It was there in his previous work of course; and always one can detect it in the varied, almost 'vocalised' sounds of his baritone-playing. But here with the Concert Jazz Band it is as if his new-developed preoccupation with lines and well-shaped contours is tending to emphasise the inherent lyricism as well.

Nowhere is this more clearly demonstrated than with his score of Django Reinhardt's *Manoir Des Mes Rêves (Django's Castle)*. The original poetry and ambiguity of the great guitarist's theme is an ideal melodic vehicle for Gerry's purposes of reconstruction, while its feeling and atmospheric awareness have encouraged his own. His finished score offers a beautifully structured unfolding of the melody at a very slow tempo — with an added personal lyricism that is intense and sensuous, never merely wistful. At the same time in his baritone solo he even manages to insert several phrases reminiscent of the way Django's fingers ran over the strings of his guitar.

To complete the picture of this Concert Jazz Band's opening book there are the straightforward swingers: *You Took Advantage Of Me*, *Broadway* and the Duke Ellington/Peggy Lee theme from *Anatomy Of A Murder*, in 3/4 *I'm Gonna Go Fishin'* . . . The LP was made in May 1960. By the time the band recorded its 'A Concert In Jazz' album just over a year later (10 and 11 July 1961) no further accusations of 'blandness' or 'a lack of push' as Gerry has since described it could truly be levelled at its output. Added to the immaculate musicianship of the earlier LP are a verve and excitement which could only evolve with a group sure of its inbuilt abilities and from players who thoroughly enjoyed being together. Mel Lewis is allowed to drive the men a vital touch harder, but the principal difference is in the ensemble attack: where cohesion and fierceness are linked in well-nigh perfect equality. Also there are more Mulligan originals on parade — although in this instance scored for the band by Bob Brookmeyer.

In fact, while Gerry got on with the everyday business of leading a big band he was actively encouraging several other talented people to write for it. Gary McFarland, then an up-and-coming graduate of the Berklee School of Music in Boston, had been invited to a band rehearsal by Brookmeyer and as a result contributed two scores. '*Weep* was the first thing Gary brought to us,' GM recalls. 'We tried it and we liked it. *Chuggin'* is a tune Gary wrote for a review. When he played it for us it sounded ideal for the band. It has a real Duke feeling.' He also persuaded his old colleague from the Miles Davis nine-piece days, Johnny Carisi, to re-score his intriguing *Israel* for the larger instrumentation. And Bob Brookmeyer arranged Gerry's *I Know, Don't Know How* and *Summer's Over*. The former had been written originally for the Mulligan Sextet, and in this later version the Sextet's last chorus has been incorporated into the writing. *Summer's Over* is another of the songs Gerry had worked on with Judy Holliday. 'It's slightly sad and wistful,' is the composer's view. 'The kind of feeling you have when Summer and the good times are gone, and Winter is coming on.' None of which has been lost on Brookmeyer, whose writing here is sensitive to an extreme.

'I think,' his leader added, 'this band feels so much like a band now that we can play pieces like these for ourselves and *feel* how they would build for an audience.' He was speaking to the magazine-writer Burt Korall. 'It (the band) is the product of seven years of thinking and trying. Typical instrumentation — seven brass, five reeds, four rhythm — didn't work out; the sound was too heavy and full. The flexibility I had been so happy with in the small group was missing. We finally came up with our current grouping — six brass, five reeds, drums and bass — which allows for variety of tone colour, and the flexibility and clarity of a small band. We actually consider the brass as five brass — three trumpets and two trombones — and a bass-trombone. Five is a lighter feeling section for ensemble sound. And the reeds actually break down to an ensemble of clarinet, alto, tenor and baritone.'

Another, outsider's view (Dom Cerulli's) becomes relevant at this point since it dwells upon the close continuing co-operation between Mulligan and Brookmeyer. It is, he wrote in 1961, 'one of the prime factors involved in the knitting together of the Concert Jazz Band. They have played together in Gerry's groups for years, and have developed an almost instinctive awareness of each other's musical thought. The small-group collaboration has extended into the Concert Jazz Band, where Brookmeyer's gutty, lyrical trombone is an important solo voice in the orchestra. In addition, Bob's writing and arranging is invaluable in setting the style and sound of the band as conceived by Gerry.'

But by a short head or perhaps even a length, the most imaginative new score to enter the band's repertoire was that produced by George Russell with *All About Rosie*. Russell, otherwise best-known in jazz circles for a method of composing called the Lydian Concept (based on an unusual scalar notation), first wrote *Rosie* as the result of a commission from Brandeis University. It is in three sections grounded on a children's play-song which Russell remembered from his youth. 'I'd asked George to write something for the band,' is how

Gerry describes what happened next. 'And when he turned in *All About Rosie*, I almost died. I was haunted by the recording he made of the piece with that fantastic piano solo by Bill Evans. But I think the band really did it well. I don't think George could get a better reading. And the way the sax section plays is terrific! *All About Rosie* may have been written originally as variations on a children's song, but I think of the three parts this way: Rosie's Early Life, Rosie's Blues and Rosie Steps Out. The way George wrote it for us, Rosie's grown up!' There are outstanding solos by the leader himself, Brookmeyer, the underrated Don Ferrara on trumpet and Gene Quill, alto-saxophone.

Despite successes like *Rosie* though, the economic conditions in the so-called Swinging 'Sixties were against Gerry's being able to keep the band going; and so now we have to take a huge leap forward in time, to the end of the 1970s, before we find him fronting another big band on a regular basis. But first, because it occurred halfway along this same time-route, I must digress to the tragedy surrounding Judy Holliday: in brief, to the last illness and death of 'an unfinished woman'.

Normally a book such as this would not need to enter into the privacies of a musician's loves and marriages. Unless, that is, as with Billie Holiday and Charlie Parker, these affairs of the heart had a tempestuous impact upon the person's career. However, Gerry Mulligan's involvement with the award-winning actress Judy Holliday turned into a musical partnership as well and thus, while it lasted, took up much of his creative time. Also, now that the facts have been revealed by Holliday's first real biographer (Gary Carey), Gerry emerges from behind them with great credit as a human being. Which, I believe, reflects back upon his music-making. For, forgetting for the moment if one can his technical virtuosity as a soloist and his overall writing abilities, a hallmark of Mulligan's music is that it is essentially happy-sounding, building up towards the passionate; or, alternately, tranquil and thoughtful turning sometimes to a moody sadness as of the blues. But never, anywhere, will one find him playing anything 'dirty' or evil-sounding — not even by clever strategy. I don't think, for instance, that he is temperamentally capable of producing the hatred (albeit an exciting hatred) of say, Howlin' Wolf Burnett's *Smokestack Lightnin'*. The Mulligan passion where it occurs is based upon warmth not anger.

He first met Judy in 1958, by which time she was already an acclaimed actress, with an Oscar for her performance in *Born Yesterday* and now, back in New York, a further triumph on Broadway in the musical, *The Bells Are Ringing*. She also happened to be six years older than he was, but in the five years of their close relationship this didn't seem to matter. She admired his talent, he had a good effect on her and in addition possessed the ability to make her laugh. He was, according to authoress Anita Loos who worked with both of them later, 'very private, quite reticent and inclined to be moody — a true black Irishman. But when he did have something to say, it was often wildly funny. He had that crazy musician's knack of giving the obvious a delicious, almost surreal slant.' Anyway, it worked for Holliday, and not only did their affair prosper but once their personal schedules allowed they began to think of writing songs together.

By the time *Bells* moved to Los Angeles Mulligan was already in Hollywood. A year earlier he had performed the music for *I Want To Live!* and was now working as an actor in *The Rat Race* for Warners. (Of his later appearance in *The Subterraneans* the less said the better; as I have already indicated.)

The songwriting seems to have got under way when in 1960 Gerry began to spend more and more time at Judy's country house in Washingtonville. He bought her a pool-table, acted as surrogate father to her son Jonathan at weekends and on weekdays, and using a small electric piano began to compose songs with her in earnest. It transpired she was a sensitive, and certainly above-average lyricist, who could express simple emotions in interestingly unorthodox ways. Their first collaboration to be performed publicly was *Blue Christmas* — by Dinah Shore on her regular TV programme.

Other work then intervened — and from around this date Judy's own career began to go wrong. It is unlikely her illness was showing yet, at least not too much; but she was the victim of much muddle and many mistakes in her theatrical career. The parts offered her were either inferior or, if they had merit, were then ruined by directors who boozed too much. Consequently the hitherto well-behaved 'star' now became temperamental. Gerry didn't interfere in any of this. He kept in the background, a quiet protector who didn't push his own opinions but was always ready with a car to pick her up. Also, he had the Concert Jazz Band to lead.

The further progress of Judy's cancer and ensuing deterioration

are fully charted by Gary Carey in his biography (see bibliography). But after her initial operation, between 1961 and early 1963, she pushed on with her songwriting and occasionally sang with Gerry. (Of the latter an LP has been released on DRG.) Their words and music, where preserved on records, reveal much to be admired — and what promised to be a major breakthrough began in 1962 when they agreed to do the score for a proposed musical based on Anita Loos' play *Happy Birthday*. Gerry rented a beach house at West Hampton and Miss Loos would join them at weekends for working sessions. 'Mulligan's music was brilliant,' the authoress said later. 'While those (Judy's) lyrics will stand up with the best of Cole Porter's and Oscar Hammerstein's or Larry Hart's.' But the producers kept calling for alterations and eventually the project fell through.

Again for reasons I don't have to go into here, the relationship between Holliday and Mulligan then foundered. But in 1965, and despite his having become involved with a younger actress, Sandy Dennis (*It's Sandy At The Beach*), once he heard that Judy was terminally ill Gerry dropped everything and largely nursed her through the final months . . .

He also quietly started paying her most pressing bills. Nor did he actually set up home with Sandy Dennis until after Holliday's death. At the funeral, wearing dark glasses, he escorted her two children. 'Not at all inappropriately,' Gary Carey concludes, 'Gerry had been granted the position of first man in her life.'

'The Wind is rising! . . . We must try to live!' Paul Valéry tells us in *Le Cimetière Marin*, the Gray's 'Elegy' of our time.

Gerry Mulligan is a workaholic because he is an enthusiast; and with the necessary patience and talent (and a little luck) this usually equals survival. But the problem for any artist of substance as he continues his efforts is to avoid being repetitive. Which is precisely why it is so stimulating to find that Mulligan's Ark of 1979 and even today has changed tack yet again. All the tangible and easily recognised features of his music are still there; but several differences have been incorporated. I also think that this is his best band so far; especially with its recording of what I consider another masterpiece — and a whole LP this time, not just a single track on an album.

Gerry Mulligan with the author. Photo: Tim Motion

Gerry was faced with a number of dilemmas when he organised this latest Orchestra, not the least of these being the problem of keeping a big band going at a time of world economic recession. Moreover, old and close associates such as Zoot and Konitz and Brookmeyer were invariably embarked on their own renewed voyages of discovery and available only for specific occasions. So the new Mulligan vessel had to be built up afresh — with the leader going for younger and relatively unknown musicians. Nothing particularly startling in this. Woody Herman has been siphoning off talented youngsters from the American colleges for years, moulding them into his annual thundering Herds. Buddy Rich's and Louis Bellson's are similarly 'blooding' bands, generally with a nucleus of veterans to steady the intake of precocious graduates. Fortunately youth is no longer a barrier to advancement in jazz — the debuts of Lee Morgan, Freddie Hubbard and now Wynton Marsalis are the most obvious testimony. Ability leading to the opportunity of an audition is the only criterion. However in Mulligan's case he would be the sole veteran; therefore he had to be sure of his aims before the new crew came aboard, following which his own proven abilities as a rehearsal leader could take over.

On the credit side though he had his fresh-sounding themes of the 1970s to draw upon, he is a good picker of men (and in this case one woman), while musically as usual he knew exactly what was wanted, even down to the set of bells his percussionist needed to travel. Stylistically the Orchestra of today has a more robust attack than any previous Mulligan group. There is more excitement generated within its ensemble and young and contrasting ideas are allowed to roam freely through the solo choruses. The important identification marks of his writing remain, with saxophones still dominating the theme statements and still frequently a baritone lead. But there are some sharper angles to the contours of his lines now, and the brasses, in punctuating these angles, are allowed to blow with a forthright brilliance not normally associated with the more mellow, integrated Mulligan sounds of previous years. However his clarity and precision are the same; and if the decibels have increased then there is also a lot of room for delicacy and a kind of magisterial gracefulness inside the overall balance. Underlining which there is always the swing — pragmatic, provoking and unadorned, undeterred no matter what the time-signature.

Grandeur of conception might appear too lavish a way of describing how Mulligan planned and built this latterday extension to his Ark. Nevertheless there are many moments when this is exactly the effect he seems to have achieved. I could cite the occasions when I heard the Orchestra in France and then in England. But there is also more positive proof with the existence of his 'Walk On The Water' LP for DRG Records.

Apart from several exotic additions to the percussion department the actual instrumentation of the Orchestra returns to that of the 1957 *All The Things You Are* sessions. Naturally though, the soloists are very different — and include several outstanding new talents. Mitchel Forman is a remarkably versatile pianist (and composer) who is clearly destined for an important future in jazz. Others whose sounds on the Orchestra's voyaging have grown distinctive include trumpeters Barry Ries and Tom Harrell, trombonist Keith O'Quinn, alto-saxist Gerry Niewood and Mike Bocchicchio on bass.

At Nice in '82 I questioned trumpeter Laurie Frink about the spirit in the band. Formerly with Machito, she has been with the Mulligan Orchestra from the outset. 'Yes, morale has remained good,' she told me. 'There have been changes of personnel, of course. But Gerry's very quick and astute when it comes to picking musicians. And although he's extremely exacting at rehearsals, he's also more than helpful in explaining things. On-stage too he's always encouraging the other players. I think he gets a great personal kick out of standing up there and hearing the musicians do something really well.' 'What was it like,' I asked her, 'touring with an otherwise all-male outfit?' She laughed. 'Strange! But not especially difficult. Everybody's equal under Gerry's leadership. I'm treated as another musician, but with the right degree of politeness. And that flag-waving number we do, the one featuring all four trumpets, I get the same solo space as the others.'

The 'Walk On The Water' LP opens with one of Mulligan's most original and arresting compositions, *For An Unfinished Woman*. The tempo is subdued, but by the conclusion — and without picking up speed — it has built up to an aggressive climax. There are several internal climaxes as well (towards the ends of individual solos) but in other places the sound dips down and the drummer sits still, thus giving the effect of a marvellous light and shade. There are dynamics too within the thematic materials. The first and recurring theme as exposed by the piano and then the brasses is a short, staccato one. But already against the brasses the leader's baritone can be heard introducing another, more flowing and legato theme — and it is this on which the improvisations are based. Again, therefore, we are presented with an illustration of how the composer can create a musical tension yielding the most satisfactory contrasts. Put simply: *Mulligan makes it work;* and in an apparently effortless manner, although the thought going into it beforehand must have been considerable. But he had at least one advantage by this date. The band's instrumentation sounds exactly right for the piece.

Song For Strayhorn has been his most popular theme from the 1970s. (Witness the applause his 1981 Yokohama performance of it gets, backed by the formidable rhythm section of Hanna, Brown and Blakey!) As well as being a tribute to the dreamy impressionism of Ellington's *alter ego* it features a melodic line truly typical of Mulligan — supple, undulating and above all easily digested by both ear and memory. Again though with his score for the band he allows in a deliberate contrast. Whereas throughout his own solo passage he maintains the stance of a balladeer, Mitchel Forman on piano is left free to switch *his* improvised ideas over to the attack. *42nd*

Gerry Mulligan on Soprano. Photo: Tim Motion

& Broadway represents Mulligan's more personal brand of impressionism. Although its chords give each soloist an opportunity to make his invention in purely jazz terms, nevertheless inside the opening theme statement (this time led by an alto-saxophone) there is an evocation of the composer's own New York; of its hurry and bustle, and with the wail of a cop-car's siren weaving through. It should be picked up by an enterprising producer and used as background music for the filming of one of Ed McBain's 87th Precinct novels.

The second half of the album begins with Mitchel Forman's *Angelica* (its melodic line almost more Mulligan than Mulligan), continues with Gerry's own waltzing *Walk On The Water*, which — like *42nd & Broadway*— carries the bonus of some soprano-playing, goes into a reaffirmation of roots and a longstanding admiration via Duke Ellington's *Across The Track Blues* and concludes with a straight-down-the-middle swinger in *I'm Getting Sentimental Over You*, something Gerry can never for long resist. The writing is consistently fine, the ensemble and solos superb and one track follows another as differing pieces fit into the pattern of an inspired mosaic. It will be a hard album to surpass. Although Mulligan being the person he is, he will no doubt try . . .

Summer 1985. And already he has gone a long way towards making me eat my words! Actually I do not rate 'Little Big Horn' (just received as an import from the U.S.) *quite* as highly as 'Walk On The Water'; but it's 'a damn near-run thing' as the Duke of Wellington might have said — and the record company could one day consider re-issuing both albums as a 2-record package. It was made in 1983, not with his regular band but with some men from it (Keith O'Quinn on trombone, Jay Leonhart, bass) and several of the top-calibre musicians on the American studio scene (Marvin Stamm, trumpet, Dave Grusin, keyboards, and Butch Miles, drums). Plus another indication that GM has been listening to the younger *avant garde* again, as demonstrated by the presence of Mike Brecker on tenor-saxophone. All the compositions are by Gerry: *Little Big Horn, Another Kind Of Sunday, Under A Star, Sun On Stairs, Bright Angel Falls* and *I Never Was A Young Man* — the first two done with an eight-piece group, the others with a quartet. His baritone is the featured solo instrument throughout, while the final track, *I Never Was A Young*

Man has the added novelty of a Mulligan vocal. And why not? I ask myself. After all he is still a musician, he sings in tune, has a pleasant sound and is thoroughly acquainted with the qualities of his own song.

However: the real strengths of the LP are those normally associated with Mulligan. The strengths of an undiminished melodic invention and logic of harmony. Very accomplished orchestration; and with plenty of rhythm, whether overt or subtle down in the engine-room of the band. And notably too great baritone-playing. As with the late Eric Dolphy on bass-clarinet, people are always having to try to measure up to Gerry's solo standards. He plays a sinewy, almost a silky thematic line on *Little Big Horn* interspersed with some tricky, choppy phrasing, but all thrown against a truly dynamic beat, with Dave Grusin proving an excellent accompanist behind GM's leads. On *Sun On Stairs* Gerry is at his most nimble and impressionistic; on *Another Kind Of Sunday* he positively revels at the head of some aggressive, but laid-back writing for the larger group. While on *Bright Angel Falls* we get more of the black gold so typical of his introspective ballad-playing. This track has something of an English modal feel about its opening statement, then moves into a slowly rocking, heavily blues-impregnated movement through the improvised parts. (Grusin follows Gerry's solo with a 'last of the whorehouse piano-players' approach, and ends doubling on concert grand with his left-hand and on an electric keyboard with his right.) *I Never Was A Young Man* is a bit of a misnomer. Gerry was a very precocious young man. He remains musically precocious well into his fifties.

Chapter Seven

Mulligan once said (4), that if he didn't get fun out of playing then he would actually much rather be a gardener. As he explained, 'That's the kind of thing — a sense of living, a feeling of continuity and relationship to the earth — which has taken me a long time to come to. It's the life that I've led and all the things I've been through that have brought me to the way I feel now. And I hate cities. When I see what happens to a city like New York — they want to put concrete from one shore of the river to the other — it's nonsense. No reason for it; it's like anti-life.'

Of course it can be argued that he has been a very successful cultivator of his own chosen ground in music. Also that his music contains a persistent enthusiasm and an awareness of roots and the main jazz tradition. At the same time though his statement does show he has thought much about his position and the links between what he does (which is cultural) and everyday life. For the more important musicians of jazz are not set apart from other people. They are of the world and in a sense they partly belong to anyone who will stop to listen.

'Music carries the message of whatever the individual who is playing it, singing it, or dancing it, has in mind,' Gerry stresses. 'That's the beauty of music, that everybody expresses *himself*. And you don't *expect* everybody to be saying the same thing. It's asking a lot of a universal language that we should all be preaching the brotherhood of man. One of the shocking realisations of true life in

(4) To Les Tomkins, of *Crescendo International*.

the world is that the concept of universal brotherhood is an intellectual ideal that, as human beings, we must strive for. Then it becomes a thing like, when you express yourself what can you do to fight for that ethic in your own time and place? But to expect everybody to feel the same way is living in some kind of bubble of unreality.

'I used to think, like a lot of us, that jazz was superior to racial prejudice and all that sort of thing. Now suddenly after all these years I'm being forced to discover that I'm White! It's the Parisians who've hipped us to the idea that there's such a thing as Crow Jim-ism. I didn't experience it when I first took my band to Paris, but I'd heard and read about it — you know, that only black men can play jazz. Well, that's going right in the face of the history of jazz and all the cats that have ever put it together, all the way back to New Orleans, Baltimore, Philadelphia, everywhere they played at the turn of the century. They were white and black, and that was the thing. Playing together, giving back and forth; it was for an individual to express himself, and it was some kind of mutual language. *Marvellous!* So it took the French to show us where the prejudice lay.

'Now the whole thing has taken on another kind of meaning. It comes to a realisation inside me that jazz is a voice to use for whatever you want to say. And a lot of young coloured cats are doing exactly that. They're relating their music to a social protest movement, the whole thing of a group of people who have been repressed and suppressed, who are trying to break out of the social bonds. Okay, so it's valid. There's no gain in saying it.

'Intellectually, you can put jazz into a little pigeon-hole and forget it, but in reality you can't do that. Because the whole concept of jazz, and what it is, relates so totally to all the music that's gone before anyway. As long as it continues to be a functional music, it will grow. You can only pour music into a dead horse for so long. In order to survive, music *has* to be functional.'

Needless to say Gerry has continued to work with black musicians. And the music itself will always come first. As it did before; as it does now in his years of maturity.

Appendix 1: The Bootleg Situation

Musicians rightly resent the existence and circulation of illegal or 'bootleg' tapes because they are deprived of both recording fees and the royalties due on all sales of their performances and compositions. Nevertheless it would be pointless trying to deny that such tapes exist. Either they have been made on small, hand-held equipment without permission at 'live' concerts — or often simply taken down from broadcasts ('airshots') or TV transmissions. Generally they remain in the possession of single collectors. Others though have found their way into a limited sales situation; hence their more serious illegality.

In Gerry Mulligan's case the most famous, or, in view of its bootleg status, notorious tape is one of the Duke Ellington Birthday Concert held at the White House on 29 April 1969. The concert is introduced by President Nixon himself and by Willis Conover and, on account of all the other taping going on inside the said House over this particular period, it seems ironic that someone smuggled a machine into the room where the jazzmen were playing.

However, after saying this, but also having heard the tape, I feel compelled to add that the occasion sounds spectacular — and it is a pity no entrepreneur has since squared it with the men in the band to get the whole thing released as a commercial LP.

For those interested, the musicians involved are Clark Terry, Bill Berry, J.J.Johnson, Urbie Green, Paul Desmond, Mulligan, Billy Taylor, Dave Brubeck, Hank Jones, Jim Hall, Milt Hinton and Louis Bellson. Together with two vocalists, Mary Mayo and Joe

Williams. All the compositions are by Ellington or Billy Strayhorn: *Take The 'A' Train, I Got It Bad And That Ain't Good, Chelsea Bridge, Satin Doll, Sophisticated Lady, Just Squeeze Me, I Let A Song Go Out Of My Heart, Do Nothing Till You Hear From Me, Don't Get Around Much Anymore, In A Mellotone, Prelude To A Kiss, Ring Dem Bells, Things Ain't What They Used To Be, Warm Valley, Caravan* and *and Mood Indigo*. The arrangements (mostly medleys) were done specially for the event by Tom Whaley, except for *Prelude To A Kiss* which was written by GM — and taken at a surprisingly quick tempo with be-bop phrasing. Meanwhile as a soloist the latter can be heard on *Sophisticated Lady, Just Squeeze Me* (playing a concluding counter melody), *In A Mellotone*, the aforementioned *Prelude, Ring Dem Bells, Things Ain't What They Used To Be* and *Warm Valley*.

For good measure Ellington receives the Medal of Freedom and the President plays *Happy Birthday To You* in the key of G.

Gordon Jack has a listing of all GM bootleg items which are *known* to exist. Apart from concerts and broadcasts by his own group and by the big band, it includes teamings with the following musicians and artists: Tony Fruscella, Mel Tormé, Don Trenner, Clark Terry, Gordon Beck, Harold Danko, Sergio Mendes, Junior Mance, Dick Cavett, Horace Parlan, Hampton Hawes, Jay McShann, Dizzy Gillespie ('The Dream Band') and Woody Herman.

Appendix 2

THE SYMPHONIC GERRY MULLIGAN
And some Conversational Notes

GERRY MULLIGAN QUARTET/LONDON SYMPHONY
ORCHESTRA
Royal Festival Hall, London, 24 October 1984

I slipped into the auditorium during rehearsals just as they were
about to embark upon *The Sax Chronicles*. *The Chronicles*, by Canadian
composer Harry Freedman, present a variety of Mulligan themes in
the styles of earlier composers as naturally as if the saxophone family
had existed for a lot longer in music; or, to be more specific and in
Freedman's chronology, according to the styles of Mozart, Brahms,
Bach, Debussy, Wagner and Richard Strauss (the waltzy Strauss of
Der Rosenkavalier).

Gerry stood very erect and calm, one hand resting lightly on the
baritone, as conductor Michel Sasson went over the notation in
certain 'key' passages. It was the first time the two men had worked
together, but clearly a mutual trust and *rapport* was developing from
the outset. Occasionally, and only occasionally, Gerry would glance
down at his own written parts; like all good players of concertos he
had the work memorised and was listening intently to the orchestra.
Nothing eluded his ears. At one point the strings took it upon
themselves to slide their mutes on. The soloist shook his head; he
wasn't going to deviate from the composer's intentions one iota and

he preferred the effect from the open strings anyway. He seemed so on top of everything that upon joining in he was undisturbed by Michel's stopping abruptly to issue fresh guidance to a particular section of the orchestra, say, the 'cellos. But in the Brahms section (based on *Milano*) he requested a slowing of the tempo. 'What you're doing sounds fine,' he told the conductor. 'It's a question of me being able to express the necessary feeling.' Such things as this were said very quietly. And still on the subject of feeling, he fully approved of Michel's idea that the brighter Bach section (which followed the Brahms) shouldn't be endangered by too much rehearsal; that it demanded a good measure of spontaneity on the night. Meanwhile the orchestral players were following everything with the closest attention. Here, their attitude suggested, was a creative player deserving of the fullest respect.

During the statutory break Gerry delayed taking one himself. He was still running over the baritone figures for the ensembled parts of the Bach, and marking the part. He also said to Michel that he hoped there'd be time for one more complete run-through of his own *Entente,* the work for saxophone and orchestra which would be opening the second half of the concert and be a European premiere. I find it reassuring to witness the keen anticipation and anxieties of outstanding performers. It confirms that nothing *blasé* has entered into the soul of their music-making.

They resumed, and at one stage during the Debussy section Gerry called across to his conductor, 'Sorry, Michel' I can't do it like that. Can you soften the orchestral effect? Otherwise it means I'll have to blow louder — then I lose all sorts of other things.'

In what he referred to as 'a trip up the Rhine', the Wagnerian-styled section based on the chorale from his 'The Age Of Steam' collection (and in this writer's opinion one of the most moving and beautiful themes he's ever written), Gerry was at his most delicate and sonorous. So much for his control though, at times, when there were just higher sustained notes, his right-hand came away from the baritone, leaving him both holding and playing the instrument with his left-hand fingers and thumb. 'What's happening in the bar before 5?' he asked Michel. 'It's uneasy there. It feels like we made a retard.' The 'cellos looked shamefaced. 'Yes, we misread it,' their leader reported.

There was another, 'safety net' run through of the chorale — then an immediate launch into the waltzy finale, which involves several Mulligan themes. Freedman has given it the full, glittering Strauss orchestral treatment, and at one point Gerry has to make a quick switch to soprano-saxophone. With which he proceeded to lay down a built-in rhythmic pulsation against the formal, swaying motion of the strings, woodwind and brass.

After this the other members of Gerry's current Quartet joined in for a rehearsal of *K-4 Pacific* (again from 'The Age Of Steam' collection). Their instruments had been set up to the left of the stage. Drummer Richard de Rosa picked up his wire-brushes and Michel Sasson called out to him. Could he move his cymbals just slightly so the two could see each other properly? Bill Mays adjusted his stool at the piano; Frank Luther sat on a higher stool, ready with his bass.

Pizzicato 'cellos and basses formed the introduction to Gerry's score, followed by a brass build-up with heavy accenting going into the essential train rhythm *per se*. The baritone solo is placed sometimes over stop-chords, at others driving very hard with a swinging 4/4 time. Only one run through was considered necessary for this piece. Again the soloist wanted to keep a freshness and excitement going. Also he had an extra score to fit in, a surprise, off-the-programme version of *Please Don't Talk About Me When I'm Gone* which would be kept on standby for an encore.

There was no time for another 'go' at *Entente*. The symphony players and Michel still had to rehearse the European premiere of Leonard Bernstein's *Divertimenti For Orchestra*, the concert's opener.

Gerry's arrival in London had come after a brief tour of Italy with his Quartet. Which in turn had followed a stay at the apartment he and his wife Franca have near Milan. For the past several years he has taken time off from all other commitments in order to write in Italy. At least two to three months each year. 'Away from the telephone and many more distractions.' *Entente* was sketched out there in four months (then orchestrated back in the U.S.); likewise a majority of his other recent compositions. Also Milan offers Gerry a further, much-appreciated bonus in addition to peace and tranquillity. 'I've become friendly with the director at La Scala,' he told me. 'So any morning I'm free there's always an open-door for me to go and listen to the opera rehearsals. It has proved a stimulating experience, especially since I always try to get a vocalised, singing quality into my own instrumental works . . .'

Where there is a true interest in his music Gerry is approachable, forthcoming and above all generous with his time; on this occasion despite his need to eat and generally prepare himself for the concert. Which was fortunate, because despite my completing the inner text of the book I still had a whole ragbag of questions to put to him — some going back to the Philadelphian and other earlier years. (Meanwhile photographer Tim Motion was stalking GM from a number of different angles, gaining close-ups.)

'*Ray:* in one of your last letters, you asked me about the Tommy Tucker band,' Gerry said. 'Well, I was with him for about three months. He liked to call us The Brass Hats. It was an ultra-commercial group, of course, and although we cut a number of demonstration discs nothing from that period was ever released. On the other hand, being with TT took me to Chicago where I spent all my time listening to the Billy Eckstine band, the seed-bed of modern jazz with Dizzy, Charlie Parker et al.'

RH: One thinks of Philadelphia being the start of your musical career, but didn't you spend some of your growing up time in Marion, Ohio?

'Yes, also a bit in Michigan. I was born in Queens Village, Long Island. My father was a management engineer and when aged nine months the family moved to Marion, where I'd stay until I was ten — hence *One To Ten In Ohio* on 'The Age of Steam' LP. My father played piano, so there was usually some music going on in the house — plus the rhythm of the nearby trains! Later in Michigan I wrote my first arrangement, based on *Lover,* for the school band. But it was turned down. I was considered too uppity and hip for one still so young.

'We moved to Philadelphia in 1944. And it was from there, in Reading, Pennsylvania, that I had my one and only teacher on clarinet and saxophone: Sam Correnti. He was a marvellous man, and it was really sad, not long ago, when we organised one of my first classical concerts which I so much wanted Sam to hear, but then he died just a couple of weeks before . . .

'But going back to your mentioning Tommy Tucker. I can remember how impressed I was in those days by the musicianship and swing of the Erskine Hawkins band. And especially the arrangements by Avery Parrish. Years later, I wrote an arrangement of *After Hours Blues* — it was right out of my head, but then I was horrified in making a comparison. I'd been copying Avery Parrish's arrangement from memory without even realising it!'

RH: Moving on now to the Miles Davis 'Birth Of The Cool' band, did all of you realise how influential it was destined to become?

'Well, maybe. We certainly believed that it meant something important — but that was only the nucleus of us. You see, some of the personnel used to change from one session to the next. For instance you mentioned Al Haig before. Well, the pianist on that session was meant to be John Lewis. But John was accompanying Ella Fitzgerald at that time, and she suddenly called a recording on the same date. Al Haig was wonderful as a jazz pianist but he didn't know our music —so all he could do was play what we put in front of him. The same thing happened with J.J.Johnson depping for Kai Winding. And I met Mike Zwerin again recently, who told me he had no idea at the time he recorded with us of the group's importance.'

RH: When you moved to the West Coast and the Gerry Mulligan Quartet took off, it wasn't very long before you had Lee Konitz guesting with the group on records. There must have been a real natural affinity going — and which enjoyed a second flowering on what we now know as your 'Gerry Mulligan The Arranger' LP.

'Lee has been creating the most beautiful improvised lines through all the years I've known him. In fact, I'll tell you something not generally known about that particular LP he made with the Quartet. At the time I wasn't too happy with my own solos or Chet's at the sessions. It was even crossing my mind that perhaps they shouldn't be released. But then I kept listening to Lee's solos on the playbacks, and they were so marvellous I decided it would be criminal not to let them go out on record. Yes, he's definitely one of the greats.'

RH: Presumably your feelings were very similar with the Sextet when you had Zoot Sims on tenor-saxophone —

'Oh, yes. Zoot and Jon Eardley and Bobby Brookmeyer. That was a band and a half. The biggest sounding small group I've ever led. Dave Bailey on drums too. He stayed with me all in all for thirteen years. Our first bass-player Peck Morrison had introduced him. I don't think I ever enjoyed touring with any other group as much.'

RH: Including the gig in Baltimore when you turned up to find the billing read 'The Gerry Mulligan Sextet featuring Brook Meyers and Soot Zims'?

He chuckled. 'It was a lousy gig too. Heavy drinkers. I don't think

Dizzy Gillespie with Gerry Mulligan at Nice '82. Photo: Tim Motion

a single one of them listened to us.'

He then agreed with my diagnosis of *The Subterraneans*.

'Sure, one of the worst pictures ever to come out of Hollywood.' But he added, 'What's even more annoying it should have been good. Mister Freed, for whom I had a lot of time, began with a script which remained very close to the original Jack Kerouac novel. Then the studio people and the money people started interfering. By the time they finished shooting there was nothing left.'

Finally — and wondering if I'd have to rewrite the end of the main text again — I asked him if there had been any more recordings under his own name since 'Little Big Horn'. 'No. You're safe for a while! And I'm going back to Italy now to do some more composing. But I have made an LP with Barry Manilow. Okay, so I was as surprised to be asked as you are to hear about it. But he contacted me, said he'd always like my playing and would I like to take some solos on his next ablum. Then I got over my surprise and did it. I think it's turned out rather well . . .'

And so to the evening and the concert itself. Bernstein's *Divertimenti* which replaced his previously advertised 'Candide' *Overture* formed a brief work written for the centenary of the Boston Symphony

Orchestra. Brassy and outgoing, they included a blues and a grand march, as well as owing certain sounds to 'West Side Story' and George Gershwin. Gerry then came on, wearing a full suit of white tie and tails, to play an extended version of *For An Unfinished Woman* with his Quartet. I never tire of hearing this, one of his outstanding themes of recent years, having now collected it with his big band, the reunion with Chet Baker at Carnegie Hall *et al.* As usual he disdained to use any microphones except one for making announcements. Which was perhaps just as well, because apart from the fertility of his improvised ideas he is also one of the most overtly *physical* of jazz players. Every sinewy melodic twist of his invention is tied to a corresponding body movement, whether an upright, majestic stance as he holds a single note or bending until his tails touch the floor in several more agitated phrases.

The first half then closed with *The Sax Chronicles*. Again I was most impressed by the Brahms and Wagner sections, but really all of the composers superimposed on one living composer proved fascinating. And of course there is scope for a sequel. Can I suggest Albinoni and either Fauré or Ravel for this?

Gerry need not have worried about an extra rehearsal of his *Entente* which came immediately after the interval. Without in any way slighting *The Sax Chronicles* (being in any case an entirely different use of the baritone) this was for me the standout of the orchestral pieces. It is a continuous work with the saxophone playing theme, variations and theme again. I was reminded of Brahms once more (the romantic feeling) and also, melodically, somewhat of Schubert in his chamber works. Gerry's scoring for the strings and woodwind was very sure, always logical and as if the baritone had been used as a concerto vehicle with large orchestral forces for centuries. Meanwhile the range and dynamics and emotions expressed via the solo instrument itself were quite formidable: an array of fine qualities like the shifting sands on a beautiful beach ending only with the far horizon. He told me over the 'phone a couple of days later that he is particularly proud of this among his recent works. He should be.

Next we had half an hour of the Quartet alone playing *Walk On The Water* and *Song For Strayhorn*, the former with Gerry on soprano throughout, demonstrating that although a latecomer to the instrument he is now its finest jazz exponent since the passing of Coltrane. The Strayhorn tribute rivals *For An Unfinished Woman* in its melodic content and likewise has been presented by Gerry through a variety of instrumental formulas. The Quartet one lives well.

Then there was a hurried council between the soloist and Michel Sasson — as a result of which they decided to do *Please Don't Talk About Me When I'm Gone* before *K-4 Pacific*. Gerry told me afterwards he hadn't realised just how short the Bernstein pieces were, and he would have preferred a different running order entirely; but as another friend remarked to me, it can't be easy to follow the 'big band' sound at the end of *K-4* when the rhythm section is driving at express speed and the brass wailing steam and red-hot coals. This was the only moment of the concert when the orchestra had a slight stumble: hitting the tempo for the final section. But within five or six bars they were together again; and when Gerry redid this section as an encore they were spot on from bar one.

A unique concert — which in its turn has left me fully reassured as to GM's future playing and composing. They're bound to be fascinating.

Bibliography

Gary Carey, *Judy Holliday, An Intimate Life Story*, Robson Books, London

Alun Morgan and Raymond Horricks, *Modern Jazz, A Survey Of Developments Since 1939*, Victor Gollancz, London

Ed.Raymond Horricks, *Jazzmen Of Our Time*, Victor Gollancz, London

Leonard Feather and Ira Gitler, *Encyclopedias Of Jazz In The 'Sixties And 'Seventies*, Quartet Books, London

At the time of writing I know of no other book devoted in its entirety to Mulligan's music. *Modern Jazz* contains some material on the Miles Davis 1948/49 band and the first West Coast Quartets; in *Jazzmen Of Our Time* Max Harrison's chapter on Gerry includes discussion of the early Sextet and also the Capitol Tentette LP. Meanwhile the 'Encyclopedias' remind us of many things GM has done in the past two decades but include the error that he actually married Sandy Dennis. Gary Carey sets the record straight as regards the latter and I recommend his book as a thoroughly good read, both for its portrayal of the beautiful, gifted and 'unfinished' actress and of Gerry as the one true adult love in her sharply curtailed life.

GM has been well served by a number of his sleeve-note writers. In France by Charles Delaunay ('The Fabulous Gerry Mulligan Quartet', Vogue) and especially the meticulous Henri Renaud ('Gerry Mulligan The Arranger', CBS). In America by Dom Cerulli

('A Concert In Jazz', Verve) — although the Verve Desmond and Hodges LP notes (by Nat Hentoff) are disappointingly facetious. (Nat Hentoff makes up for this with a good chapter on Mulligan in his book *Jazz Is*.)* In GB I like the pieces written by Alun Morgan for the 'Lionel Hampton Presents Gerry Mulligan' LP (Kingdom Jazz) and the one made in Italy with Enrico Intra (PRT/Pye). Plus of course Les Tomkins' interviews with GM for *Crescendo International*.

Finally too there is a long and detailed assessment of the Quartet and Tentette recordings with Chet Baker by Pete Welding. This accompanies the new boxed set of all their Pacific Jazz sessions together with a number of previously unreleased items. The 63-title project was researched by Michael Cuscuna, but Welding's essay makes valuable reading for its track-by-track account of everything Mulligan laid down with Baker and also Lee Konitz in the period 1952/53.

* More recently too there are the superior notes by Ira Gitler for the 3 'Mainstream' LP reissues by the GM Sextet on Emarcy.

Selected Discography

I have based my selections on records generally available at the time of going to press and further listening suggestions follow the main discography. The following abbreviations have been used: (arr) arrangement; (as) alto-sax; (b) bass; (bars) baritone-sax; (cl) clarinet; (cond) conductor; (p) piano; (sop) soprano-sax; (tb) trombone; (tp) trumpet; (ts) tenor sax; (vbs) vibraphone; (vcl) vocal; (vtb) valve trombone; all other instruments given in full. Locations: LA Los Angeles; NYC New York City. Only records issued in (Eu) Europe and (Am) United States of America are noted. If a record is only currently available in (J) Japan, this too is noted.

TONY MIDDLETON *London*, February 1986

ELLIOT LAWRENCE AND HIS ORCHESTRA
1946 – Hindsight (Am) HRS182. Three 1945 Gerry Mulligan scores including INDIANA reported to be Mulligan's first paid arrangement.

GERRY MULLIGAN THE ARRANGER
CBS (Eu) 82273. 1946/7 arrangements for Gene Krupa, playing and arranging with Elliot Lawrence 1949 plus 1957 recordings with his own orchestra.

THE BIRTH OF THE COOL
Capitol (Eu) CAPS1024. 1949/50 recordings with the Miles Davis Orchestra. Mulligan arranged JERU, GODCHILD, VENUS DE MILO, ROCKER and DARN THAT DREAM.

GERRY MULLIGAN
Jerry Hurwitz, Nick Travis (tp); Ollie Wilson (tb); Allen Eager (ts); Max McElroy (bars); Gerry Mulligan (bars, arr); George Wallington (p); Phil Leshin (b); Walter Bolden (d); Gail Madden (maracas)–1.

NYC. August 27, 1951

171	ROUNDHOUSE	Prestige OJC 003
172	IDE'S SIDE–1	,,
173	BWEEBIDA BOBBIDA–1	,,
174	KAPER–1	,,
175	FUNHOUSE–2	,,
176	MULLENIUM–1, 2	,,
177	MULLIGAN'S TOO–1, 2	,,

Note: all titles arranged and composed by Mulligan. Max McElroy plays the second baritone solo on MULLENIUM and does not play on Mulligan's too. Omit brass–2.

Gerry Mulligan recordings June 1952 to June 1953: All recordings for Pacific Jazz including BERNIE'S TUNE, LULLABY OF THE LEAVES, NIGHTS AT THE TURNTABLE and WALKIN' SHOES, a Tentette date for Capitol (1/53), plus many previously unissued takes are in a five LP set issued in America on Mosaic records. Not readily available in the UK but further details from Mosaic Records, 1341 Ocean Avenue, Suite 135, Santa Monica, California 90401, USA.

GERRY MULLIGAN QUARTET
Chet Baker (tp); Gerry Mulligan (bars); Carson Smith (b); Chico Hamilton (d). *LA.*
September 2, 1952

9258	LINE FOR LYONS	Prestige (Eu) 68350
9261	CARIOCA	,,
9266	MY FUNNY VALENTINE	,,
9271	BARK FOR BARKSDALE	,,

same as September 2, 1952.   *LA. January 3, 1953*

1315	LIMELIGHT	Prestige (Eu) 68350
1316	THE LADY IS A TRAMP	,,
1326	TURNSTILE	,,
1327	MOONLIGHT IN VERMONT	,,

Note: other titles on 68350 same as OJC 003.

GERRY MULLIGAN QUARTET
Bob Brookmeyer (vtb); Gerry Mulligan (bars); Red Mitchell (b); Frank Isola (d). *Paris, France. June 1954*
MOONLIGHT IN VERMONT, COME OUT WHERE EVER YOU ARE, FIVE BROTHERS, WALKIN' SHOES, LOVE ME OR LEAVE ME, THE LADY IS A TRAMP, BERNIE'S TUNE, LAURA, UTTER CHAOS, LINE FOR LYONS, SOFT SHOE, BARK FOR BARKSDALE, MY FUNNY VALENTINE, TURNSTILE, THE NEARNESS OF YOU, MOTEL, I MAY BE WRONG, LULLABY OF THE LEAVES, MAKIN' WHOOPEE.

Vogue (Eu) VJD504

Note: the above titles recorded in concert at Salle Pleyel, Paris during the period June 1 to 7, 1954.

GERRY MULLIGAN SEXTET

Jon Eardley (tp); Bob Brookmeyer (vtb, p); Zoot Sims (ts); Gerry Mulligan (p, bars); Peck Morrison (b); Dave Bailey (d).   *NYC. September 21, 1955*

12044-1	BERNIE'S TUNE	EmArcy (J) 195J-33
12045-1	MUD BUG	,,
12046-1	BLUES	EmArcy (J) 195J-35
12047-1	THE LADY IS A TRAMP	,,
12048-3	DUKE ELLINGTON MEDLEY (Moon mist/	
	In a sentimental mood)	EmArcy (J) 195J-37
12049-1	DEMANTON	EmArcy (J) 195J-35

same as September 21, 1955.   *NYC. September 22, 1955*

12050-1	APPLE CORE	EmArcy (J) 195J-33
12051-4	BROADWAY	Emarcy (J) 195J-35
12052-5	SWEET AND LOVELY	EmArcy (J) 195J-33
12053-1	SWEET AND LOVELY	EmArcy (J) 195J-35
12054-5	BERNIE'S TUNE	,,
12060-5	WESTWOOD WALK	EmArcy (J) 195J-37
12061-3	BLUES	,,
12061-2	BLUES	EmArcy (J) 195J-35

same as September 21, 1955.   *NYC. October 31, 1955*

12296-4	BROADWAY	EmArcy (J) 195J-33
12296-5	BROADWAY	EmArcy (J) 195J-36
12297-1	DEMANTON	,,
12297-12	DEMANTON	EmArcy (J) 195J-37
12298-6	NIGHTS AT THE TURNTABLE	EmArcy (J) 195J-33
12299-1	EVERYTHING HAPPENS TO ME	EmArcy (J) 195J-36
12299-2	EVERYTHING HAPPENS TO ME	,,
12299-4	EVERYTHING HAPPENS TO ME	EmArcy (J) 195J-33
12300-2	THE LADY IS A TRAMP	,,
12300-4	THE LADY IS A TRAMP	EmArcy (J) 195J-36

GERRY MULLIGAN SEXTET

Jon Eardley (tp); Bob Brookmeyer (vtb, p); Zoot Sims (ts); Gerry Mulligan (p, bars); Bill Crow (b); Dave Bailey (d).   *NYC. January 25, 1956*

12428-5	WESTWOOD WALK	EmArcy (J) 195J-36
12429-17	AIN'T IT THE TRUTH	EmArcy (J) 195J-34
12430-2	MAINSTREAM	,,
12431-8	LA PLUS QUE LENTE	EmArcy (J) 195J-36

same as January 25, 1956 except Don Ferrara (tp) replaces Jon Eardley.

NYC. September 26, 1956

14179-2	LA PLUS QUE LENTE	EmArcy (J) 195J-37
14180-8	IGLOO	EmArcy (J) 195J-34
14181-2	MAKIN' WHOOPEE	EmArcy (J) 195J-37

14182-3	ELEVATION	EmArcy (J) 195J-34
14183-3	LOLLYPOP	,,
14381-1	BLUES AT THE ROOTS	,,

GERRY MULLIGAN QUARTET
Bob Brookmeyer (vtb); Gerry Mulligan (p, bars); Joe Benjamin (b); Dave Bailey (d).
Sweden. May 17, 1957
WALKIN' SHOES/MY FUNNY VALENTINE/BLUES AT THE ROOTS/BERNIE'S TUNE   Ingo (Eu) SIX
Note: other titles refer 1966. above titles recorded in Stockholm.

GERRY MULLIGAN with TEDDY WILSON TRIO
Gerry Mulligan (bars); Teddy Wilson (p); Milt Hinton (b); Specs Powell (d). *Rhode Island. July 6, 1957*
SWEET GEORGIA BROWN   Verve (Eu/J) MV2622

GERRY MULLIGAN QUARTET
Bob Brookmeyer (vtb); Gerry Mulligan (bars); Joe Benjamin (b); Dave Bailey (d).   *Rhode Island. July 6, 1957*
UTTER CHAOS/MY FUNNY VALENTINE   Verve (Eu/*J) MV2622*
Note: the above recordings took place at the Newport Jazz Festival. Other titles on MV 2622 do not feature Gerry Mulligan.

GERRY MULLIGAN—PAUL DESMOND QUARTET
Paul Desmond (as); Gerry Mulligan (bars); Joe Benjamin (b); Dave Bailey (d).
NYC. August 1, 1957
Verve (Eu) 2304329

21221	BODY AND SOUL	Verve (Eu) 2304329
21222	BLUES IN TIME	,,
21224	WINTERSONG	,,

Note: other titles refer August 27, 1957.

GERRY MULLIGAN—THELONIOUS MONK QUARTET
Gerry Mulligan (bars); Thelonious Monk (p); Wilbur Ware (b); Shadow Wilson (d).   *NYC. August 12, 1957*
STRAIGHT, NO CHASER   Milestone (Eu) 68136
STRAIGHT, NO CHASER (alternate take)   ,,
RHYTHM-A-NING   ,,
I MEAN YOU   ,,
I MEAN YOU (alternate take)   ,,
I MEAN YOU (alternate take
        to previous)   ,,

same as August 12, 1957. *NYC. August 13, 1957*
DECIDELY Milestone (Eu) 68136
DECIDELY (alternate take) "
'ROUND ABOUT MIDNIGHT "
SWEET AND LOVELY "
Note: other titles do not feature Gerry Mulligan.

GERRY MULLIGAN—PAUL DESMOND QUARTET
Paul Desmond (as); Gerry Mulligan (bars); Joe Benjamin (b); Dave Bailey (d).
NYC. August 27, 1957
21323 FALL OUT Verve (Eu) 2304329
21324 LINE FOR LYONS "
21325 BATTLE HYMN OF THE REPUBLIC "
21326 STANDSTILL "
Note: other titles refer August 1, 1957.

GERRY MULLIGAN—STAN GETZ QUINTET
Stan Getz (bars -1, ts); Gerry Mulligan (ts -1, bars); Lou Levey (p); Ray Brown (b);
Stan Levey (d). *LA. October 22, 1957*
21700 THAT OLD FEELING Verve (Eu) MV2657
21701 THIS CAN'T BE LOVE "
21702 BALLAD "
21703 SCRAPPLE FROM THE APPLE Verve (Eu) MV2661
21704 I DIDN'T KNOW WHAT TIME IT WAS "
21705 LET'S FALL IN LOVE –1 Verve (Eu) MV2657
21706 TOO CLOSE FOR COMFORT –1 "
21707 ANYTHING GOES –1 "
Note: other titles on MV2661 do not feature Gerry Mulligan.

ANNIE ROSS with THE GERRY MULLIGAN QUARTET
Chet Baker (tp); Gerry Mulligan (bars); Henry Grimes (b); Dave Bailey (d); Annie
Ross (vcl). *LA. February 11, 1958*
HOW ABOUT YOU/THIS TIME THE DREAMS ON ME/LET THERE BE LOVE/ BETWEEN THE
DEVIL AND THE DEEP BLUE SEA/IT DON'T MEAN A THING
World Pacific (Spain) WP1253

GERRY MULLIGAN QUARTET
Art Farmer (tp); Gerry Mulligan (bars); Bill Crow (b); Dave Bailey (d).
Newport.R.I. July 6, 1958
AS CATCH CAN CBS (Eu) 88605
BERNIE'S TUNE FDC (Eu) 1024
BAUBLES, BANGLES AND BEADS "
LINE FOR LYONS "
Note: 88605 is a double LP. Other titles on 88605 and 1024 do not feature Gerry
Mulligan.

ANNIE ROSS with THE GERRY MULLIGAN QUARTET

Art Farmer (tp); Gerry Mulligan (bars); Bill Crow (b); Dave Bailey (d); Annie Ross
(vcl).   *LA. September 25, 1958*
I FEEL PRETTY/GIVE ME THE SIMPLE LIFE/I'VE GROWN ACCUSTOMED TO YOUR FACE/
THIS IS ALWAYS   World Pacific (Spain) WP1253

THE NEW GERRY MULLIGAN QUARTET

Art Farmer (tp); Gerry Mulligan (bars); Bill Crow (b); Dave Bailey (d).
                                                            NYC. December 17, 1958
CO 61956   BLUEPORT   CBS (Eu) 88041

as previous.   *NYC. December 18, 1958*
CO 61972   MY FUNNY VALENTINE   CBS (Eu) 88041

as previous.   *NYC. December 23, 1958*
CO 60207   UTTER CHAOS   CBS (Eu) 88041
CO 60209   AS CATCH CAN   "

as previous.   *NYC. January 15, 1959*
CO 61954   JUST IN TIME   CBS (Eu) 88041
CO 61955   WHAT IS THERE TO SAY?   "
CO 61956   FESTIVE MINOR   "
CO 61957   NEWS FROM BLUEPORT   "
Note: other titles refer June 1962.

GERRY MULLIGAN—BEN WEBSTER QUINTET

Ben Webster (ts); Gerry Mulligan (bars); Jimmy Rowles (p); Leroy Vinnegar (b);
Mel Lewis (d).   *LA. November 3, 1959*
22973   CHELSEA BRIDGE   Verve (Eu) 821167
22974   GO HOME   "
22975   WHO'S GOT RHYTHM?   "

same as November 3, 1959.   *LA. December 2, 1959*
23006   TELL ME WHEN   Verve (Eu) 821167
23008   THE CAT WALK   "
23009   SUNDAY   "

GERRY MULLIGAN—JOHNNY HODGES QUINTET

Johnny Hodges (as); Gerry Mulligan (bars); Claude Williamson (p); Buddy Clarke
(b); Mel Lewis (d).   *LA. July 1960*
BUNNY/WHAT'S THE RUSH/BACK BEAT/WHAT'S IT ALL ABOUT/18 CARROTS FOR
RABBIT/SHADY SIDE   Verve (Eu) 2304476

GERRY MULLIGAN AND THE CONCERT JAZZ BAND
Nick Travis, Doc Severinsen, Don Ferrara (tp); Bob Brookmeyer (vtb); Willie Dennis, Alan Ralph (tb); Gene Quill (as, cl); Bob Donovan (as, flu); Jim Reider (ts); Gene Allen (bars, bs-cl); Gerry Mulligan (bars, p); Bill Crow (b); Mel Lewis (d).   *NYC. July 10/11, 1961*
ALL ABOUT ROSIE/WEEP/CHUGGIN'/I DON'T KNOW HOW/SUMMER'S OVER/
ISRAEL   Verve (Eu) 2304424

GERRY MULLIGAN—PAUL DESMOND QUARTET
Paul Desmond (as); Gerry Mulligan (bars); John Beal (b); Connie Kay (d).
                                                                    NYC. June 26, 1962
N2PW1668   THE WAY YOU LOOK TONIGHT   RCA (Eu) CL42788
N2PW1669   BLIGHT OF THE FUMBLE BEE   ,,
Note: other titles refer July 3 and August 13, 1962.

GERRY MULLIGAN QUINTET
Gerry Mulligan (bars); Tommy Flanagan (p); Ben Tucker (b); Dave Bailey (d); Alec Dorsey (conga).   *NYC. June 30, 1962*
CAPRICIOUS/HERE I'LL STAY/INSIDE IMPROMPTU/YOU'VE COME HOME/
GET OUT OF TOWN/BLUE BOY/LONELY TOWN   CBS (Eu) 88041
                    Note: other titles refer December 1958, Jan 1959.

GERRY MULLIGAN—PAUL DESMOND QUARTET
Paul Desmond (as); Gerry Mulligan (bars); Wendell Marshall (b); Connie Kay (d).   *NYC. July 3, 1962*
N2PW1665   ALL THE THINGS YOU ARE   RCA (Eu) CL42788
N2PW1670   STARDUST   ,,

same as July 3, 1962 except Joe Benjamin (b), Mel Lewis (d) replace Wendell Marshall and Connie Kay.   *NYC. August 13, 1962*
N2PW1671   TWO OF A MIND   RCA (Eu) CL42788
N2PW1672   OUT OF NOWHERE   ,,

GERRY MULLIGAN SEXTET
Art Farmer (tp, flh); Bob Brookmeyer (vtb); Gerry Mulligan (bars, p); Jim Hall (g); Bill Crow (b); Dave Bailey (d).   *NYC. September 1962*
29347   NIGHT LIGHTS   Mercury (Eu) 6336345
29348   WEE SMALL HOURS   ,,
29349   FESTIVE MINOR   ,,

same as September 1962.   *NYC. October 3, 1962*
29384   MORNING OF THE CARNIVAL   Mercury (Eu) 6336345
29388   TELL ME WHEN   ,,
29390   PRELUDE IN E MINOR   ,,

From this point up to 1966 Gerry Mulligan recorded a number of LP's for the Limelight label, none of these are currently available.

GERRY MULLIGAN QUINTET
Gerry Mulligan (bars); Burt Adams (p); Dean Wright (g); Eddie Gomez (b); Dave Bailey (d).
1966
LULLABY OF THE LEAVES/BODY AND SOUL/ALL THE THINGS YOU ARE
Ingo (Eu) Six

Note: other titles refer May 17, 1957.

From the mid sixties to the early seventies Gerry Mulligan worked with Dave Brubeck, recording for Columbia and Atlantic. None of these recordings are currently available.

Another currently unavailable but excellent recording for A & M in 1971. *The Age of Steam*, A & M (AM) SP3036.

GERRY MULLIGAN—CHET BAKER
Chet Baker (tp); Ed Byrne (tb); Gerry Mulligan (bars); Dave Samuels (vbs, percussion); Bob James (p, elp); John Scofield (g); Ron Carter (b); Harvey Mason (d).
NYC, November 24, 1974

LINE FOR LYONS	CTI (Eu) 6054
FOR AN UNFINISHED WOMAN	"
MY FUNNY VALENTINE	"
SONG FOR STRAYHORN	"
IT'S SANDY AT THE BEACH	CTI (Eu) 6055
BERNIE'S TUNE	"
K-4 PACIFIC	"
THERE WILL NEVER BE ANOTHER YOU	"

GERRY MULLIGAN—ENRICO INTRA ENSEMBLE
Gerry Mulligan (bars); Giancarlo Barigozzi (sop, flu); Enrico Intra (p); Sergio Farina (g); Pino Presti (b); Tullio De Piscopo (percussion).
Milan, Italy, October 16/17, 1975
NUOVA CIVILTA/FERTILE LAND/RIO ONE/CHAMPOLUC   Pausa (Am) PR7010

GERRY MULLIGAN'S NEW SEXTET
Gerry Mulligan (sop, bars); Dave Samuels (vbs); Tom Fay (p); Mike Santiago (g); George Duvivier (b); Bobby Rosengarden (d).
NYC, late 1976
IDLE GOSSIP/STRAYHORN 2/WALK ON THE WATER/WALTZING MATHILDA/OUT BACK OF THE BARN/NORTH ATLANTIC RUN/TARUS MOON
Chiaroscuro (Am) CR155

GERRY MULLIGAN—LIONEL HAMPTON
Gerry Mulligan (bars); Lionel Hampton (vbs); Hank Jones (p); Bucky Pizzarelli (g); George Duvivier (b); Grady Tate (d); Candido Camero (conga drums). *NYC. October 29, 1977*

APPLE CORE/SONG FOR JOHNNY HODGES/BLIGHT OF THE FUMBLE BEE/GERRY MEETS
HAMP/BLUES FOR GERRY/LINE FOR LYONS
Kingdom (Eu) GATE7014

Note: Two additional titles from the above session, LIMELIGHT and WALKIN' SHOES
are on GATE7015. These do not feature Lionel Hampton.

GERRY MULLIGAN AND HIS ORCHESTRA
Laurie Frink, Barry Ries, Tom Harrell, Mike Davis (tp); Keith O'Quinn, Dave
Glenn, Alan Ralph (tb); Ken Hitchcock (as, ts); Gerry Niewood (as); Gary Keller
(ts); Ralph Olsen, Seth Brody, Eric Turkel (saxs); Joe Temperly (bars); Mitchel
Forman (p); Jay Leonhart, Mike Bocchicchio (b); Richie Derosa (d); Gerry Mulligan
(sop, bars, arr).

NYC. September 1980
FOR AN UNFINISHED WOMAN/SONG FOR STRAYHORN/42ND & BROADWAY/ANGELICA/
WALK ON THE WATER/ACROSS THE TRACK BLUES/I'M GETTING SENTIMENTAL OVER
YOU   DRG SLC5194

GERRY MULLIGAN
Gerry Mulligan (sop, bars, keyboards); Dave Grusin (keyboards); Tom Fay (p,
fender rhodes); Peter Levin (moog synthesizer); Edward Walsh (oberheim synthesizer); Derek Smith (p); Jack Six, Jay Leonhart (b); Michael DiPasqua, Bobby
Rosengarden (percussion).

Connecticut, 1982
DANCE OF THE TRUCK/INTROSPECT/WATCHING AND WAITING/TRUCKING AGAIN/
NEW WINE/THEME FROM "LA MENACE"/VINES OF BORDEAUX/THE HOUSE THEY'LL
NEVER LIVE IN/WATCHING AND WAITING (reprise)/THE PANTOMIST/INTROSPECT
(reprise)/VINES OF BORDEAUX (reprise)
                                                       DRG (Am) MRS506

GERRY MULLIGAN
Gerry Mulligan (bars, vcl); Dave Grusin (synthesizer, electric p, p) Jay Leonhart
(b); Buddy Williams (d).

NYC. 1983
I NEVER WAS A YOUNG MAN vGM   GRP (Am) A1003
UNDER A STAR   "

as previous, add Richard Tee (p).
BRIGHT ANGEL FALLS   "

as previous, omit Tee and Butch Miles (d) replaces Buddy Williams.
SUN ON STAIRS   GRP (Am) A1003

NYC. 1983
Marvin Stamm, Alan Rubin (tp); Keith O'Quinn (tb); Lou Marini (as); Michael
Brecker (ts); Gerry Mulligan (bars); Dave Grusin (p, electric p); Anthony Jackson
(b); Buddy Williams (d).

NYC. 1983
LITTLE BIG HORN/ANOTHER KIND OF SUNDAY   GRP (Am) A1003
Note: The above LP won a Grammy award.

Titles of LPs in the main discography

OJC 003	*Mulligan plays Mulligan*
68350	*Mulligan/Baker — 2 LP*
VJD504	*The fabulous Gerry Mulligan Quartet*
Ingo SIX	*Gerry Mulligan Vol 2 Live in Stockholm*
195J-33	*Presenting Gerry Mulligan Sextet*
195J-34	*Mainstream of Jazz*
195J-35	*Mainstream of Jazz Vol 2*
195J-36	*Mainstream of Jazz Vol 3*
195J-37	*A profile of Gerry Mulligan*
MV2622	*Teddy Wilson trio and Gerry Mulligan Quartet at Newport*
2304329	*Blues in time*
68136	*Thelonious Monk/Gerry Mulligan 'round midnight*
MV2657	*Getz meets Mulligan in Hi-Fi*
MV2661	*Stan Getz-Gerry Mulligan and Stan Getz-Oscar Peterson*
88605	*Newport Jazz Festival (Unreleased highlights from 1956, 1958, 1963)*
FDC 1024	*Newport Jazz Festival 1958-59*
WP1253	*Annie Ross sings a song with Mulligan*
88041	*My funny valentine*
821167	*Gerry Mulligan meets Ben Webster*
2304476	*Gerry Mulligan meets Johnny Hodges*
2304424	*A concert in Jazz*
CL42788	*Two of a kind*
88041	*Jeru*
6336345	*Night lights*
CTI6054	*Carnegie Hall Concert Vol 1*
CTI6055	*Carnegie Hall Concert Vol 2*
PR7010	*Gerry Mulligan meets Enrico Intra*
CR155	*Idle gossip*
Gate7014	*Lionel Hampton meets Gerry Mulligan*
SLC5194	*Walk on the water*
MRS506	*'La Menace O'*
GRPA1003	*Little big horn*

Further Listening Suggestions

GERRY MULLIGAN LIVE IN STOCKHOLM, MAY 1957. INGO (Eu) Three.

JAZZ GIANTS 1958. Mulligan, Stan Getz, Harry Edison plus the Oscar Peterson Quartet. Verve (J) MV2540

RECORDED LIVE AT RENAISSANCE CLUB, LA. 1959. with Ben Webster and Jimmy Witherspoon. Joker (Eu) SM3279

THE CONCERT JAZZ BAND: LIVE AT THE VILLAGE VANGUARD NYC 1960. Verve (J) MV2592. On tour with guest soloist Zoot Sims, 1960, Verve (J) MV2653. New York December 1960, Musidisc (Eu) JA5236. Judy Holliday, Holliday with Mulligan, DRG (Am) SL5191

MULLIGAN ARRANGEMENTS PLAYED BY VIC LEWIS AND HIS ORCHESTRA. Mole (Eu) 9

MULLIGAN ARRANGEMENTS PLAYED BY CLAUDE THORNHILL AND HIS ORCHESTRA. MCA (J) 3147

MULLIGAN ARRANGEMENTS PLAYED BY ELLIOT LAWRENCE AND HIS ORCHESTRA. Fantasy (J) LPJ40008

THE SOUND OF JAZZ: December 1957 TV show; also Columbia record date with Gerry Mulligan part of an all star band backing Billie Holiday singing 'Fine and Mellow'. Also as a member of Count Basie All Stars.

TANGO NUEVO – GERRY MULLIGAN/ASTOR PIAZZOLLA, MILAN, 1974. Adantic (Am) ATL 50168

BARRY MANILOW: 1984 recording with popular American vocalist. Also features Sarah Vaughan, Mel Tormé and Shelly Manne. Arista (Eu) 206496.